"His fans love his tongue-in-cheek, affectionate and personalized novels."

—**The *New York Times***

"Part entertainer, part psychotherapist. An online celeb whose star quality leaps from the screen."

—*USA Today*

"His stories, frequently a combination of fact and fiction, can be oddly touching and seemingly dead-on. He has a gentle touch and, his fans insist, a poet's soul."

—*Wired*

"It was the Great American love story—simple, honest, innocent and with a happy ending. And as writer Dan Hurley read it to Melissa Grigoruk, on whose life the fictional account was based, the glow on her face and the sparkle in her eyes revealed the awesome power of love. 'It was beautiful, wonderful,' said the twenty-five-year-old Bethlehem woman, who was touched by its simplicity and originality."

—*Allentown Morning Call*

"A Cyrano for tongue-tied children of all ages has appeared in our midst."

—*New York Daily News*

"On a recent spring evening at 63rd Street and Broadway in Manhattan, it didn't take long before a small crowd clustered around Hurley. After a few probes, Dan was ready to write about a couple named Carla and Jay. His fingers flew. No erasing. Sixty seconds later, more or less, Dan reached the end of the novel. He read the novel aloud. When he was finished, Carla wept. 'He got to the heart of what little he knew,' she said, 'and he was kind.'"

—*Newsday*

"A sidewalk Shakespeare."

—*People*

"Since Dan Hurley launched 'The Amazing Instant Novelist' on America Online, he's attracted thousands of loyal followers to his quirky smorgasbord of humor, poetry and 60-Second Novels."

—Crain's New York Business

"He calls them '60-Second Novels' because they take him barely a minute to write, and because they re-create in miniature the themes of a novel—a moment, a problem, a victory, or even a fantasy, in the lives of his customers. All are tinged with the gentle irony that is Hurley's trademark. Being a 60-Second Novelist has taught him a lot about life. And as everyone knows, life can be stranger than fiction."

—The Record (New Jersey)

"He aims to 'kick the literary establishment in the knees,' he says. And 60-Second Novels are his first step to turn writing back into something that has an impact on people's lives."

—The Christian Science Monitor

"Care to have a go at naming history's most prolific creator of fiction? No, it's not Shakespeare or Cervantes or any political speech writer. Underachievers all, compared to Dan Hurley. During the past thirteen years, this amiable New Jerseyite has authored more than 17,000 novels. Hurley is a sidewalk Steinbeck, a pavement Proust, a storefront Freud."

—Fort Worth Star-Telegram

"The 60-Second Novelist has gone from street corner to the party circuit to the online world. Fans can't get enough. One of the first celebrities to emerge from the online services."

—Baltimore Sun

"'60-Second Novelist' tops bestseller list in cyberspace."

—Bangor Daily News (Maine)

"Ignoring the amused skepticism that greeted what he freely acknowledges is a nutty idea, Hurley took typewriter to street and started typing. And then he discovered cyberspace. Hurley pulled onto the information Superhighway and became a star."

—The Star-Ledger (New Jersey)

The 60-Second Novelist

What 22,613 People Taught Me About Life

Dan Hurley

Health Communications, Inc.
Deerfield Beach, Florida

www.hci-online.com

Triple image of Dan, all chapter title pages, ©Greg Vimont.

Rockin' Dan with computer keyboard, pages 33 and 183, ©Norman Y. Lono.

Dan underwater on front cover and on pages 33, 67, 68 and 110, by Doug Max.

Dan and Alice toasting each other, pages 33 and 42, ©Ellen DeBoise.

Dan at party (with models Laura McKeown, left, Brian Dunleavy and Celia Vimont) on cover and pages 33 and 97, ©Greg Vimont.

Dan at party, page 34, ©Greg Vimont.

Dan with duck, pages 67 and 68 by Doug Max.

Dan "shocked," pages 97, 107 and 108, ©Greg Vimont.

"Eureka," front cover, pages 107, 121 and 131, by Dan Hurley.

Portrait of Joel Mollon, pages 121 and 140, by Dan Hurley.

"Drive Thru," pages 121 and 124, by Alice Hurley.

Louisa May Alcott's grave, page 150, by Dan Hurley.

"Tall Story" video images, pages 163–182, by Richard Reta.

Shakespeare at computer, page 183, ©Greg Vimont.

Main screen and logo of "Amazing Instant Novelist" site, page 184, designed by William R. Rayl.

Library of Congress Cataloging-in-Publication Data

Hurley, Dan
    The 60-second novelist / by Dan Hurley.
      p. cm.
    ISBN 1-55874-692-7
    1. United States—Social life and customs—20th century Fiction.
2. Fiction—Technique. 3. Performance art. I. Title. II. Title: Sixty-second novelist
PS3558.U5328. A614 1999
813'.54—dc21
                                      99-24529
                                          CIP

©1999 Dan Hurley
ISBN 1-55874-692-7

Publisher: Health Communications, Inc.
              3201 S.W. 15th Street
              Deerfield Beach, FL 33442-8190

Cover and book design by Larissa Hise
Inside book layout by Dawn Grove
Cover photographs of Dan Hurley in yellow suit by Greg Vimont

For Alice

Contents

Acknowledgments

So many people have been important to the development of this book, but none more so than the 22,613 people over the past sixteen years who participated in the creation of their 60-Second Novels. Without their willingness to try something they didn't quite understand, to tell their story to some guy with a typewriter, this book would not have been possible.

My literary agent, Jane Dystel, saved the book from being just a neat idea. Her tenacity and honesty are greatly appreciated.

I gratefully acknowledge that parts of chapter 1 were previously published in *Whole Earth Review* and *Writer's Digest*, parts of chapter 7 in *Good Housekeeping*, and parts of chapter 8 in the *New York Times*.

Invaluable critical insights from Lee Quarfoot, fiction editor of *Good Housekeeping*, and Jean Graham, former *Woman's Day* senior editor, helped me to find the book's final structure.

Longtime members of my monthly writers' group—Janet Bailey, Erica Manfred, Norman Schreiber, Minda Zetlin, Toni

Kamins, Kim Flodin, Florence Isaacs, Joan Iaconetti, Marian Betancourt and others who have come and gone—have been a continuing source of encouragement and support. Members of my writers' groups in St. Louis and Chicago, including Dwight Bitikofer and Rhea Hilkevitch, helped me to keep believing in my dreams when they were little more than figments of my imagination.

Nan Gatewood gave important editorial advice on early versions of "60 Seconds in the Life of America."

At the American Society of Journalists and Authors, executive director Alexandra Owens, and past president Mark Fuerst, helped to make "Tall Story" more than just a tall tale. The friendship and assistance of Brian Dunleavy was also critical to the success of the event.

At America Online, among the dozens of executives I've worked with, I especially thank Danny Krifcher, Ted Leonsis, Ruby Warren, Martha Girard, Miguel Monteverde, Jeff Bellin, Jesse Kornbluth, Mary Lynne Ashley and Clay Buckley. I also thank Steve Case for building such an awesome literary playground.

My "Amazing Instant Novelist" site would not survive a day without the brilliant, superhuman work of my site manager, William Rayl. Bill, you are the best.

For saving the site from oblivion, I thank John White and Johnny Michaels. I'll never forget that drive down to AOL through the Storm of the Century.

Staff manager Patricia Rayl has somehow managed to keep nearly two hundred people from across the United States avoid virtual pandemonium. Senior managers Rhonda Perrett, Mary Ellen Rogers, Barbara Quinn and Patricia R. Piatt have stuck like Krazy Glue for over three years, and I could never thank them enough for all they've done. To all the other staffers, as well as the fans: your devotion and enthusiasm have been . . . amazing!

I especially thank those staffers who reviewed and rated the hundreds of 60-Second Novels I considered including in the book: Alisa Scheps, Ruth Egan, Kathleen Koelble Hingel, Barbara Hicks, Roberta Nolte, Dina Robinson, Eric Sagel, Loralee Peterson, Mike McReynolds, Sandi Morgan, Debbie Santano, Rick Light, Kathy Corcoran, Marie Falco, Anita Clare, Doris Phillips Doud, Marge Garnett, Debi Staples, Amanda Dunn, Barbara Quinn, Debbie Paliagas, Jackie Gingrich, Laura Moore, Silvia M. Vincent, Elaine Clausen, Deb Andoetoe, Steve Tessmer, Jan Soares, Anne Jasper and Elise Holm. Many visitors to the site also read and rated the stories, and all your contributions made a critical difference in separating the wheat from the chaff.

If Kim Weiss at Health Communications hadn't been so enthusiastic about my book proposal, I doubt it ever would have been published. To her and publisher Peter Vegso, I say thanks for going with your gut and making a lifelong dream come true. I am indebted to editors Christine Belleris and Allison Janse, who helped transform that rickety proposal into something I can be proud of; their patience and skill are extraordinary. And Larissa Hise's design of the book has made it a thing of beauty.

Special teachers along the way include Alice Kihn, Mr. Bogan, Terry Reidy, the late Joe Edwards, Tom McBride and Robert Karen.

To my mom, Mary Hurley, thanks for all your years of hard

work and love. To my brothers, John, Michael, David and Patrick; my sister, Eileen; my grandmother, Agnes; my cousins, nieces, nephews and other family members: I love you all very much. And to the memory of my deceased father David: I hope they have a bookstore up in heaven, Dad!

To my lifelong friend, Dan Feigelson: without you, there never would have been a Bob Cat, and without a Bob Cat, there never would have been a 60-Second Novel.

To my darling daughter, Annie: "I tubby you."

Finally, to the woman who dated me when I didn't have enough to pay for her drinks; who was proud of me even when I made my living on the streets; who read countless drafts of countless versions of books based on the 60-Second Novel; who took me out for champagne at the Algonquin when I published my first article in the *New York Times*; who came along when I wanted to write my way across the country, and ordered pizza when I decided to write from the roof of a skyscraper: Alice, you are my muse and my inspiration, and I love you with all my heart.

Author's Note

Many of the 60-Second Novels in this book are verbatim, published here the way I wrote them in a minute or two (or three, or five) for people on the streets, at parties, in department stores or on America Online. Others have been lightly edited, either to remove a stray phrase, fix a funky line or get a fact straight. Except in those cases where a person's last name is included, all names and other identifying details have been changed to protect privacy. Such tinkering might be considered cheating under Jack Kerouac's strict standards for what he called "spontaneous prose." But the heart of a 60-Second Novel is not that it *was* written spontaneously, but that it *is* written interactively, *right now*, based on a brief conversation with *you*. Until you come and get yours, this book will have to do.

Dan Hurley
April 20, 1999

In the future everyone will be world-famous for fifteen minutes.

—Andy Warhol, catalogue of his photo exhibit in Stockholm, 1968

To make sense of their span, [people] need fictive concords with origins and ends, such as give meaning to lives and to poems.

—Frank Kermode, "The Sense of an Ending"

It had at this time become my custom—and it still is my custom, though of late I have become a little lenient to myself—to write with my watch before me, and to require from myself 250 words every quarter of an hour.

—Anthony Trollope, *Autobiography* (1883)

Museums, to me, border on funeral parlors. I'm not saying you can't learn from museums. But my work, to be fulfilled, needs the interaction of people. What I'm trying to do is get sculpture off the pedestal and into the street.

—Richard Serra, quoted in the *New York Times Magazine*, October 8, 1989

Zola called it documentation, and his documenting expeditions to the slums, the coal mines, the races, the folies, *department stores, wholesale food markets, newspaper offices, barnyards, railroad yards, and engine decks, notebook and pen in hand, became legendary. At this weak, pale, tabescent moment in the history of American literature we need a battalion, a brigade of Zolas to head out into this wild, bizarre, unpredictable, hog-stomping Baroque country of ours and reclaim it as literary property.*

—Tom Wolfe, "Stalking the Billion-Footed Beast," *Harper's*, November 1989

The more words one uses the greater is the emptiness of it all.

—Ecclesiastes 6:11

Brevity is the soul of wit.

—William Shakespeare, *Hamlet*

Chapter 1

What 22,613 People Taught Me About Life

L et me tell you a story. Back in 1983, when I was twenty-four years old and working in Chicago as an editor at the American Bar Association, I wanted nothing more than to become a novelist. In the mornings I awoke at six o'clock to write my novel. In the evenings, I sometimes stood up, mid-conversation with friends, and announced that I'd just had an idea and had to go home to write.

Then one October morning on the bus ride to work, a coworker and I were trying to think up Halloween costumes. I hit on a ridiculous idea: "How about if I went as a writer, with a typewriter slung from my shoulders, and walked around the party like one of those old-fashioned cigarette girls, saying, 'Short stories? Poems? Novels?'"

My coworker, Mary, laughed and said, "You've got to do it, Dan!"

"Definitely!" I replied. And never did. Of *course* I never did. What was I, *nuts*?

But the idea haunted me all that winter and into spring. I

began thinking it would be cool to do it on a street corner, as performance art (or performance *writing*). Something about the idea grabbed me: writing in public, on demand. Ridiculous, absurd, silly—but interesting. And behind the absurdity, I sensed the possibility of touching people more directly with my writing than I ever had while sitting alone at my desk. Heck, if nothing else, it would make a good story to tell my grandchildren.

One night when I lay in bed trying to sleep, battling the usual "maybe I should try it" thoughts, I climbed out of bed, sat at my desk, switched on the lamp, took a yellow legal pad and tried to see if my idea wasn't so crazy that I couldn't figure out a way to make it work. The first problem I saw was the weight of my typewriter. I picked up the big, gray, manual Royal from the 1950s and realized immediately that it was far too heavy to walk around with it hanging from my shoulders. Then I remembered the folding director's chair in the back of my kitchen closet: maybe I could just sit there on the sidewalk with the typewriter in my lap.

I went into the closet and pulled the chair out, dusted it off and sat down with the typewriter in my lap. It felt heavy, but rested squarely and securely on my knees. It worked.

What would I call it? Thinking of the bestselling book, *The One-Minute Manager*, I made a little sign to tape on my typewriter so people would see it as they walked by:

60-SECOND NOVELS
Written While You Wait

That Thursday night, I met with my monthly writers' group and tried it out on them, asking each a few questions, and then spontaneously typing a few sentences inspired by our conversation. "So, what'd you think?" I asked, looking around the room like a dog waiting to be petted.

"Well, Dan," said my friend Bob, "it's kind of weird."

But I didn't mind; that was the whole point. I did fear getting arrested, laughed at or just ignored. I even pictured the frightening possibility of a man grabbing my typewriter and throwing it at me. But the fears were part of what made my experiment so interesting. I was heading into uncharted wilderness, and if a map of what lay ahead had been available, I wouldn't have bothered taking the trip.

So on Sunday, April 24, 1983, at about 2 P.M., I carried my twenty-eight-pound 1953 Royal typewriter atop the fabric seat of my folding director's chair through the stiff wind of Chicago's Michigan Avenue, and set up in front of the Old Water Tower. I had dressed in my three-piece gray flannel suit, blue-and-gold tie, white Oxford button-down shirt and black wingtips—the outfit I normally wore to my job at the ABA—to counteract people's automatic assumptions that a man sitting on the sidewalk with a typewriter in his lap had to be insane or begging for money. When I reached a spot where the sidewalk was widest, I opened up the folding chair, sat down with the typewriter in my lap and taped my "60-Second Novel" sign to the back of it so that it faced the passersby.

For the first minute, I felt totally ridiculous, as if I were sitting there naked. "Would you like a 60-Second Novel?" I forced myself to ask a middle-aged man walking by.

"Not today," he replied.

Instantly I blurted back, "How about tomorrow at five-thirty?"

He laughed but kept walking. Now another feeling stole over me: freedom, abandonment. I had no idea what I was doing, and I had never felt more alive.

Not knowing what else to do, I slipped a piece of paper (and carbon paper for making a copy) into the typewriter, and began typing the world's first 60-Second Novel, which I here reprint in its entirety, typos and all:

```
One day Dan Hurley got this crazy idea to
go out on Michigan Avwmu3 to see what would
happen if he began typing on the street.
 People walked by and laughed.   He felt
sort of strange.  Wouldn't you?
```

I didn't know what to do with it. "Excuse me, sir, would you like a 60-Second Novel?" I asked a young man walking by. He didn't reply. I asked a few more people, and they ignored me too. Finally I stood up, set the typewriter on the chair and walked over to a middle-aged woman in a business suit, who was waiting for a bus.

"Ma'am, would you like this story I just wrote?" I asked.

"All right," she said reluctantly, as if I were handing her a flyer for a strip joint.

I sat back down and shivered in the wind, inviting whoever passed to get a 60-Second Novel. The whole thing took on the aspect of a psychological experiment. I was a human Rorschach. No one knew what I was doing there, least of all me, and so everyone had to invent an explanation, assign me a meaning.

Some laughed cynically and said, "What a gimmick," as though I had thought the whole thing up as a money-making scheme. Others looked sympathetic and said, "A starving poet!" One elderly lady asked me if I were selling the typewriter. A couple walked by, and the woman asked her husband, "What's he doing?" The man answered, "He's trying to get a job." Sitting there watching people watch me, I could almost see their minds whirring and clicking as they tried to find a single pigeonhole where "writer" and "on the street" could fit together.

After getting either ignored, misunderstood or laughed at by everybody who walked by for half an hour, I watched an elderly couple walk toward me and then stop in their tracks, pointing and laughing. Another couple of boneheads, I figured. And then the woman spoke.

"I don't know what you're doing," she said, "but whatever it is, I want one!"

The man added, with a wry smile, "It certainly is something extremely unusual."

I looked them up and down—their eyes glistened with excitement, they had huge grins, they looked totally enchanted—so I just asked their names and began writing:

Something Extremely Unusual

It happened one cloudy afternoon. They had been walking on Michigan Avenue, George and Mitzy, when suddenly they became...ALIVE! It couldn't have ever been expected. The first thing Mitzy noticed was that she was breathing, that her heart was beating, that she was walking on Michigan Avenue. She suddenly realized that fox for all the box years that the world had been going on, all the billions of eons, she had been dead. And now, suddenly, for a spark of a moment, she was alive.

George was devestated by the knowledge that this was his life, his one and only life, that he was living right now. He could feel his skin sweating. He could hear the sound of his breathing in his own ears. He could actually SEE things. He could actually HEAR sounds. Yes, it was the most unusual thing, to be alive. Because so many people are dead. So many. They live in the past. They dwell on tomorrow. They think angry thoughts about other people. They try to get somewhere. They lose themselves. They forget the crucial fact that they are alive. And when you forget it, you are dead. And so to be suddenly alive, that is the strangest, the most unusual, the most bizarre thing in the world. To really live. To really be alive. To be fully alive. Living. Hooray life. Hooray for living people. They're so extremely unusual.

Dan Hurley

As I typed, I noticed shoes crowding toward me on the sidewalk. Whispers and chuckles came from behind my back. Someone jostled my elbow, and a toddler began pawing at the carriage return. When I finally  pulled the page out of the typewriter, I looked up to see about twenty-five people surrounding me, blocking off the sidewalk so that others had to walk into the street to get around.

"Read it!" shouted a few of them.

I read it. When it was over, they applauded.

"Where do I put the money?" asked George.

"Money?" I repeated.

"Who's next?" asked a thirty-something guy in the crowd. "Is there a line?"

In that moment—I still remember the sight and sound of that crowd as though they were standing around me now—the entire direction of my life veered off-road. It was my first experience of "eureka!" I had no idea what I had discovered—or what had discovered me—but I could see it worked. And so I wrote another. And another.

Rather than embarrassing me or scaring me into silence, the crowd spurred me into a creative frenzy. They were the ultimate deadline. Words leapt from my brain to my fingers with barely a pit stop in my awareness. Time shrunk down to a dustball. The world transformed into words.

Seven stories later, my fingers stiff from the cold, the crowd having ebbed away, I packed up to leave. The last thing I did before lugging my typewriter back to the car was to count my earnings for the hour: $14.75. Eureka indeed.

My life took on a Clark Kent-Superman split: mild-mannered reporter for the American Bar Association by day, 60-Second Novelist fighting a never-ending battle for literature and tips by night. At first, I charged like a museum: Pay what you wish but you must pay something. Most people gave me a dollar or two, sometimes five dollars or ten dollars. One guy gave me twenty-five dollars and a bottle of Bailey's Irish Cream. Another gave me ten dollars and a condom (unused). When I decided to fix the price at two dollars, suddenly more people wanted them. They were valuable now because they cost money.

That first summer, I feared I was turning into a Stupid Human Trick: "Dan Hurley, the human story machine: Put in a word, he spits out a story!" I also feared that I'd soon get bored. (Sixteen years and 22,613 novels later, I'm still waiting.) But it seemed that no matter what I wrote, people laughed, or sometimes cried, and thanked me till my ears were ready to fall off. Many told me they were framing their stories. I received cards and letters from across the United States. At least one woman a night kissed me and more than a few gave me their phone numbers.

The longer I kept at it, the more people opened up to me, pouring out their life stories and their problems, taking me more seriously than I took myself. Maybe it was my innocent "cub reporter" looks. Maybe it was my genuine fascination with what they had to say. Or maybe people were just dying

to open up to somebody, anybody, and I just happened to be the first guy they found sitting on the street with a typewriter. Clearly, though, they needed something they weren't getting from psy- My Chicago Street Performer License. chotherapists, clergy, family or friends. And so they gave me their trust. I, in turn, gave them stories that were neither fiction nor nonfiction but some hitherto unknown confection of fact, fiction, fable, bibliotherapy, Socratic dialogue and Dear Abby. "Only connect," E. M. Forster once wrote, and that's what we did.

But before I typed even a single word, I gave them something else: my ears and my eyes, my total 200 percent attention. And there's precious little more in this world that people really want.

To draw them out, I asked questions. Nosy questions, personal questions, questions you're not supposed to ask.

"Why should I tell you?" some would demand, unintentionally revealing their cautious, suspicious nature. Everything they said, or did not say, revealed their personality and their life. Everything about a person, I realized, is of a piece: their shoes, their friends, the words they use. The parts express the whole. Follow any thread, you get to the heart.

No matter what people confessed, I listened without judgment and without opinion. I listened to a married secretary who was having an affair with her boss and who wanted to give him a love note. I listened to a mentally ill man who literally thought he was Elvis. I listened to a businessman in a gray suit as he broke down crying about his impending divorce. Children and crack addicts, the homeless and the famous, schizophrenics and astronauts, mayors, movie stars, millionaires and one confessed murderer—I listened to them all as they told the messy, mixed-up, jumbled-up truth of their lives.

Early one evening in August, a young man came up, introduced himself as Albert, and started talking without my even asking. To him it seemed that a guy with a typewriter sitting on the sidewalk was the most natural thing in the world. I listened as he told me of his unemployment, his pregnant girlfriend, his search for an apartment. "I'm going through a lot of changes," he said, after twenty minutes of yakking. "I'm pretty shook up in life right now. Right now I'm going to pray to God. I'm thinking of praying to God."

Eventually Albert wandered off with the story I'd written for him (gratis), and as I sat there watching the passersby, a thought began to percolate in my brain. Picture the scene: about sixty people walked by each minute (I counted), about one each second. Some trudged, lost in their thoughts, looking down at the sidewalk, not even seeing me. Others paraded along in their evening gowns and tuxedos, laughing, having the time of their life. And suddenly it dawned on me that all of these people, no matter who they are—sixty a minute, thirty-six hundred an hour, nearly thirty thousand in a typical evening—everybody was living a life of unfathomable meaning and complexity. Millions and millions of them. And there I was to listen and write it down. Not for the rich and famous, but for the average and the ordinary; not for the mass media of the millions, but for the micro medium of one person at a time: a direct communication between writer and reader, instantly and on the spot, without interference by publishing conglomerates.

I've since devoted my life to writing these novels from Chicago to New York, as far

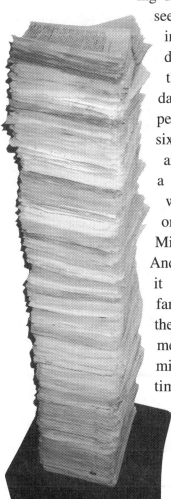

The carbon copies of all 22,613 stories I've written stand in a stack over four feet tall.

west as Hawaii, north to Canada and south to Florida—on streets and online, at department stores and trade shows, at bars and bar mitzvahs. At this point, there aren't enough seats in Madison Square Garden to fit all the 22,613 people I've written for. But from the very first day, I kept a carbon copy of each story I wrote. The pile of tissue-thin copies now stands over four feet tall here in my study. They're colored white and green and pink and blue and yellow—a rainbow of stories, a pillar of life's little lessons.

After all these years and all those stories, the question I still find myself puzzling over is: Why on earth did this crazy, absurd, goofy gimmick work so far beyond anything I had imagined?

On the simplest level, I know people have always enjoyed seeing my typewriter—first the Royal, and now the portable 1937 Remington that I use, which in today's world of laptops looks like an antique. How fast I type on it and the noise of the old thing is another neat part of the appeal. (I've never been clocked, but I am wicked fast.) And while everyone has seen an athlete or a singer perform, it's unheard of to see a writer perform—not by reading, but by writing on the spot. Being drawn into that process by which a writer takes the "facts" and transforms them into a story is a kick. There's just no getting around the Stupid-Human-Trick aspect to it all.

But I like to think there's something more, something that speaks to the incredible power of the life stories we tell ourselves about ourselves. We *need* our life stories for our very survival. Stories are like those little microbes in our guts, the ones that help us digest food. If we didn't have little stories in our brains, how else could we digest our lives?

But ironically—and this is one of the most important lessons I've learned—all 22,613 of the people I've written for were bigger than their stories. Whether it was some hot-shot wealthy vice president of a corporation, a housewife or a homeless person, I could always see beyond the story. I could look them deep in the eye, crack a smile and somehow both of us knew without saying it, "We're just two kids, making up stories about ourselves, playing make-believe."

That's the beauty of very small children: Stories to them are a game, a toy to be played with, while the real treasure is this magic moment. Soon after my daughter, Annie, began to walk, she was always stopping to look at things. She couldn't pass a store window without looking at it and asking, "Whaddat?" She'd see a crack in the sidewalk and say, "Whaddat?" The faded, cheesy display in the liquor store window of a cardboard woman holding a six-pack—Annie would stop in front of it and say, "Look, Daddy!"

She had no story. She simply *was*. She was *present* every-where we went. The story I had in my head—that we were walking *to the diner*—that didn't occupy Annie. She was just *walking*.

Living minute by minute, in the moment: that's the pot of gold at the end of the rainbow. To quote a 60-Second Novel I wrote in 1985 for a woman named Evelyn: "In the real world, happy endings don't just happen to us. We write our own happy endings, by creating our own happy present right now." And that, as best as I can figure it, is the whole enchilada.

And so what follows are just over sixty of my favorite 60-Second Novels, each of them written on the spot in response to a story that someone told me. As for my own story: Not only did my crazy idea to write stories on the street bring me a career, it brought me my wife, Alice (whom I met while writing her a 60-Second Novel), and I guess you could say my dream of becoming a novelist also came true. Not quite the way I'd expected—writing novels on the street, one page in length, for one person at a time. But then no good story turns out the way you expect.

Chapter 2

Man on the Street

After taking a week's vacation to see what it would be like to write on the streets of Chicago for seven days straight in the spring of 1984, I ended up earning over twelve hundred dollars. The next day I told my boss at the American Bar Association that I was quitting to become a full-time 60-Second Novelist.

I spent that first full-time week testing out the sidewalks of New York. I'd grown up in New Jersey, and had always hoped to return to the area. Whereas in Chicago I had been a freak, in New York I discovered that I was just one more street performer in a rapidly growing Sidewalk  Vaudeville. Saturday night on

Columbus Avenue, I competed for space with mimes, magicians, break-dancers, balloon twisters, palm readers, fire-eaters, portrait artists, a guy who played a harpsichord on wheels, a woman who played the flute, and a father-daughter tap dance team. Even so, 60-Second Novels worked as well with the hardened New York crowd as it had with the humble Midwesterners.

Sidewalk Psychiatrist

On the Monday before I planned to return home to Chicago to pack and move permanently, two pretty young women walked up to me at the corner of Columbus Avenue and 72nd Street. They introduced themselves as Amy and Susan.

"Out shopping?" I asked.

"We're on day leave from the psychiatric floor of a hospital," said Amy.

"Seriously?" I asked.

"Very seriously," said Amy, with a sad look in her eyes.

"But is life really so bad?" I asked.

"Sometimes I just forget about the good," said Susan, "because there's so much bad."

They looked so young, so fresh-faced and innocent, I felt I had to try writing something that would inspire them and remind them of how good life can be. And so I wrote:

The Forgetting Sickness
and the Remembering Recovery

Amy and Susan had this thing where they
kept forgetting.

They would wake up in the morning and
forget ik about the smell of a lake in the
woods at dawn in the autumn. They would forget about being held by another human being.
They would forget the feeling of getting
really excited about something coming up,
something big like Christmas, or something sa
small like waiting for dinner to be served.

Or they would forget the sound of geese
going north in the spring. They would forget
the taste of coffee in the morning when you
wake up, and how the shower feels when you
get in and it starts waking you up, and you
push the bar of soap over you and your skin
starts to tingle.

They forgot all sorts of things, like love
and friends and hope. They forgot hearing
all the traffic, joking with other people on
the street.

Then they went to a place where doctors
helped them to remember. And slowly now they
are starting to remember.

But as they remember all these beautiful
things, they also begin to remember the pain
and the trauma and the difficulties, which is
why they forgot the beautiful things in the
first place.

But that is life. The pain AND the
beauty, the good AND the bad.

And so we hang onto the beauty and the
love and the happiness, we hang on strong,
and remember it.

Remember these good things.

Remember to remember.

Two days before Christmas that year, I received this post-card from Susan, which she had sent to the address photo-copied on the bottom of her novel:

Dear Mr. Hurley:

I, and my friend Amy, were clients of yours one day in July/August—we were hospital patients @ the time. We're both out now—we're both trying to be "good." I'm writing you because I think you should know that all of Unit 5 loved and was inspired by the story you wrote for us, "The Forgetting Sickness and the Remembering Recovery," and I wanted to thank you on everyone's behalf, and also just for me, because you gave me a very "bright" memory on that day, and some pleasure, and a lot of other subtle possessions of a beautiful memory. I hope your writing is a source of joy to you, and I hope whatever project you are working on is going along well.

Thank you, Susan

Taste of Chicago

After my one-week test of New York, I returned to Chicago to pack and move for good. The weekend of July 4, I performed at "Taste of Chicago," an outdoor food festival packing over 100,000 Midwesterners into a park the size of a football field. They crowded around me and dripped mustard down my back and spilled beer in my lap and waited for their novels as though I were grilling hamburgers. I felt like the Ray Croc of literature, the Henry  Ford of writing. I was on an Assembly Line of the Mind, offering Fast Food for Thought. The second day it rained—and I kept right on writing. That night a group of boys pickpocketed me of about fifty dollars from my back pocket. I chased them, but then I returned to my typewriter— and kept on writing. Nothing could stop the presses. I typed so quickly, and with so little time for planning a plot, that the stories had to write themselves. I felt lifted up and taken over by the flood of words.

On the afternoon of July 4, a man named Silas walked up with a woman and a child.

"Are you married?" I asked.

"We are one family," he said, and that was all I needed:

WE ARE ONE FAMILY

Silas motioned to his wife and child
and said, "We are one family." There was
a grandeur to his words, a power. He spoke
boldly and chose his words xxx well. Yet
Silas did not know the full distance that
his words traveled. Because when he motioned
to Sherri, his daughter, who loves playing
the piano, and when he motioned to Elnora,
who loves going to church because it helps
to fulfill her life--when he motioned to
these two, and said, "We are one family," I
saw beyond him the crowd standing around us
at the Taste of Chicago, I saw the bums and
the vendors, the businessmen and the taxi
drivers, I saw the whole city of Chicago, I
saw xxx with the sweep of his arm that he
included all of Illinois, the cornfields and
the cities, the goats and the geese and the
farmers and the truckers, I saw him include
in xx his strong arms the whole country,
celebrating its independence today, and I
saw the Communist countries, and the people
starving, the poor in Africa and the rich in
their castles, the sheep herders and the
xxxxxxxxxx aborigines, the French and the
German and all living things on Earth, and I
saw his hand sweep farther still, to include
Venus and Mars and the Sun, straight beyond
to the outer edges of the galaxy, the quasars
and the starx systems and all of God's
world, I saw him include everything, because
it is as he spoke, "We are one family."

The Reader Who Slapped Me

In what other form of literature can the reader literally reach out and slap the writer?

On the afternoon of July 5, at the height of "Taste of Chicago," two teenage girls walked by, looked at me, and one said derisively to the other, "That looks like a queer way to make a living." Her friend stopped and said, "I don't know; it looks like a good way to earn a living." They talked about it for a moment and then decided to have their story written.

A half-hour later, the one who had originally derided my writing—I'll call her Lydia for the purposes of this story—returned with a guy. "Lydia doesn't like her novel," he told me. I guess I was supposed to be intimidated, but he was a pip-squeak. "She wants another one."

"It was stupid," Lydia said. "You just repeated what we said to you."

I was in the middle of typing another story for someone else, though, and a line of people were waiting for theirs. "I'll give your money back," I volunteered, "but I can't write you another one. I liked the one I wrote you."

She wouldn't take no for an answer, so she stood in front of me for about twenty minutes, yelling at anyone who passed. "He really stinks!" she told people. "Don't get one." But no one paid her any mind. She became like a carnival barker for me.

Finally, to settle the matter, I offered to read the story aloud to the crowd that surrounded us, and let them be the judge of whether it was any good or not. She agreed.

I read it aloud, and everyone applauded. They said they liked it.

Still Lydia wouldn't give in. Finally a break in the line came.

"Are you really sure you want another one?" I asked her. "I don't think you'll like it." I said this because after writing about two hundred novels in three days, looking into the hearts and souls of so many people, I felt more like an oracle or a psychic than a fiction writer, and was in no mood to write a cutesy little story to pacify Lydia.

"Yes, I'm sure," she said. "Write me a new one."

I gazed into her eyes, feeling almost out of my body, as though the truth itself were speaking through my typewriter, as my fingers typed out the following:

Dear Lydia:
I'm sorry that you have nothing better
to do than get mad at people on the street.
That's what bag ladies do, they get angry
at nobodies, they yell at figments of their
imagination.
Does something from your past still annoy
you? Was there some time in your life
when someone did something rotten to you
that you're still walking around with? I
recommend that you give it up, let it go,
and start enjoying life.
See me?
See me sitting here?
I'm having fun.
I hope you are too.
But no, you prefer to stand here and
waste the entire day being angry. WHAT
POSSIBLE POINT IS THERE IN REMAINING HERE
IF YOU'RE NOT HAPPY WITH THIS? WHY KEEP
COMING BACK FOR MORE?
Let it go. Have a beer. Enjoy
yourself. In ninety years, no more, you'll
be dead. And either you will have enjoyed
your life. Or you will have stood around
yelling at people who made you mad.
What's your choice?

                    Very sincerely,

                    Dan Hurley

Lydia insisted on reading her 60-Second Novel aloud to the crowd. She started with an ironic tone, as though laughing at my words. By the end, though, she had to use a more authentic, dramatic voice, to show the crowd that she was in on this, that she already understood what I was saying. When it was over, she left without another word.

A minute later, she was back. She shrieked at me for another ten seconds, then suddenly slapped me across the face.

I stood up. "You're going to have to leave immediately," I said, "or I'm going to call the police." She left.

A half-hour later, her girlfriend came back alone. "I just wanted to tell you," she said, "that everything you said about Lydia was right."

Even so, this taught me that people are capable of hearing only so much. I vowed never to confront someone so aggressively again. I wanted to touch people—not get into fistfights with them.

Sidewalks of New York

I moved to New York and wrote on the streets all summer long: weekdays in midtown, weekend afternoons at South Street Seaport or the Metropolitan Museum of Art, and evenings on the Upper West Side. Late one night in Manhattan on Columbus Avenue and 72nd Street, two middle-aged guys with long black hair walked up.

They looked like a couple of regular joes—one kind of skinny, the other with a bit of a beer belly, both in T-shirts.

"Write us a story about a bar called 'Warm Beer and Lousy Food,'" said the skinny guy with a beak of a nose. "That's all we're telling you. Just write."

This one inspired me:

SELF EXPRESSION

Once upon a time, there was a man
who was an utter failure at everything,
because he kept trying to be a success.

At heart, he was not a success. At
heart, he was a failure, and because he
kept trying to succeed, he kept failing
worse and worse.

So finally he gave up and decided to
express his sense of failure and outrage
at the world. He opened a bar called
"Warm Beer and Lousy Food."

The public flipped for it. They
loved the audacity of it, the sheer
absurdity and straight-forwardness of it.
Plus, it was so damn different. So damn
unique.

They realized it was the perfect
expression of one man. He had finally
expressed perfectly his sense of
failure.

And as a failure, he became a great
success.

They laughed and gave me ten dollars—twice my new price.

As they walked away, the guy with the beer belly turned back and said, "You know who you wrote that story for? Alice Cooper."

The moment he said the name, I recognized rock 'n' roll's beak-nosed bad boy, the forerunner to today's Marilyn Manson.

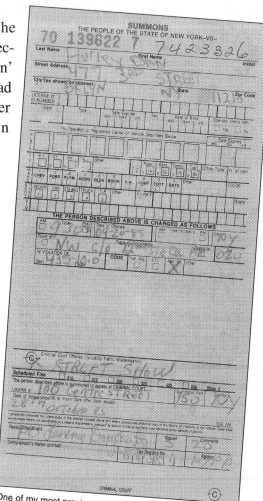

One of my most precious possessions: a ticket I received in 1985 for writing novels on the sidewalks of New York. Where was my poetic license when I needed it?

On Sunday, September 30, 1984, in front of the Metropolitan Museum of Art, a happily married couple in their thirties named Darrell and Olga told me the question he'd asked her when they first met fifteen years earlier:

HOW LONG WILL THIS TRAIN BE DELAYED?

Darrell was on the Number 7 train, trying to go on with his life. He thought life would be as unsettled and directionless as it had always been for him.
Then the train stopped between stations. "Excuse me," he said to Olga, a young woman standing next to him. "Do you know how long this train will be delayed?"
Now he truly saw her. She was a big woman, a whole lot of woman, and a whole lot of what he liked. She had nice full lips and big brown eyes and beautiful brown hair and a happy smile. She was from Central America. Darrell was the exact opposite: He had a European background, and he was pale and small. It was Mr. and Mrs. Jack Spratt all the way.
He could feel the magic. From that very first instant, Darrell knew they would get married and live happily ever after.
But first Olga had to answer his question. She had to tell him how long this train of life would be delayed from the dead end he had been heading toward. And Olga answered: "Forever."

Chapter 3

Have Remington, Will Party

I soon became a regular performer on New York's glittering party circuit, which was growing only more lavish with every junk-bond takeover. Instead of the gritty sidewalks, I worked at places like the Park Plaza, the Pierre, the Helmsley Palace, a holiday party in the home of Katharine Graham, a bar mitzvah on the lavish QEII, and another that took over the entire Madison Square Garden. Corporations and individuals flew me to California, Canada, Florida and Fort Worth.

Amidst the pomp, I found myself in the position of a real-life Nick Carraway, the fictional character to whom everyone confesses their inner secrets in F. Scott Fitzgerald's novel, *The Great Gatsby*. Behind the tuxedos and taffeta, I learned, these were the same people I'd been interviewing on the streets.

Lost and Found

At a party in the New York Hilton for the American Formalwear Association in 1985, I met a couple who told me that their story was "weird, wild and wonderful." And so I wrote:

```
              The Three W's


     Frances Neuman and Bob Young grew
up together in a Chicago orphanage in
the 1940s.  They became sweethearts,
and in seventh grade Frances would bake
cookies and put them in his desk drawer,
which was better than his under drawers,
which the  nuns never would have allowed.
They never even kissed, these two. Holding
hands was as far as things got.  They both
turned sixteen, and Bob took a job outside
the orphanage.  They parted and never saw
each other again.
     Bob was almost married three times,
when he was twenty-five, thirty and thirty-
five.  Each time the woman backed out.  The
last time he felt a sense of relief and gave
up trying to marry.  He reached his fifties
single, running "Be Young Formalwear" to
supply tuxedos to other people's weddings.
     Frances married a wonderful man named
Kenneth, and they had three beautiful kids.
Then, after twenty-four years together,
Kenneth died.  At first Frances was sure
she would never want to remarry, and then
she just forgot about it, and likewise
crossed into her fifties alone.
```

Then the orphanage gave a reunion, and thirty-eight years after Bob and Frances last saw each other, they met again. Bob knew immediately that it was love all over again.

"Since you dance the polka so well," he said to her on the dance floor, "how about if I take you out to lunch?"

They talked till four in the morning on their first date. Frances felt as nervous as a kid. On their second date, Bob finally said that he loved her. Frances was leery, but he was just the way he'd been years ago: courteous, kind and considerate. She thought, "This can't be true."

But now it's been three years that they've been Wildly, Weirdly, Wonderfully happy together. And on November 22, they will get married. Bob figures that after supplying formalwear for 50,000 weddings, what's one more?

And the nuns will just have to look the other way when he kisses the bride.

Bob and Frances Neuman on their wedding day.

Mother and Child Reunion

At a law firm's holiday party on Tuesday, December 22, 1998, a middle-aged woman named Barbara told me that nine years earlier, she had donated a kidney to her daughter, Deborah. The donated kidney had functioned well for seven years, but in 1996 Deborah had to go back onto dialysis. I asked Barbara what she thought of the Arizona convict, recently in the news, who wanted to donate his second and last kidney to his daughter. "If it wasn't illegal, I would do it too," Barbara said, even though Deborah would remain in good health on dialysis until another kidney become available. I asked why Barbara would be willing to risk her own life to give her daughter a kidney. Her answer became the title of her story:

GIVING BIRTH A SECOND TIME

Barbara and her husband, Ben, have one child, a daughter named Deborah.

They had wanted to have more, but it was God's plan that they would have just one. Barbara would have liked to give Deborah brothers and sisters. They would have had six if they could. But God had other plans.

Deborah turned out to be a dynamic, strong-willed, personable young woman-- just totally wonderful in Barbara's eyes.

But she also turned out to have systemic lupus, which caused her kidneys to fail. She was on dialysis for two years until finally the doctors xxxx announced she had end-stage renal disease. At that point, Barbara knew the opportunity had come to give birth again.

This time, she did it by giving one of her kidneys to Deborah, in an operation in 1989 that took five hours. The moment Barbara's kidney was xx placed in Deborah, it functioned perfectly. For Barbara, the operation was like giving birth a second time, giving her daughter a second chance at life. She felt total elation. And nothing would please her more than if she had a dozen more kidneys, so she could just keep giving birth over and over.

Dan Hunley

At a party in a Soho loft, I saw an elderly man with a long white ponytail. I figured he had to be some kind of flaky aging artist, but he turned out to be the total opposite of flaky.

```
               HONEST ABE

     Abe is honest.  He's a man of his word.
As a CPA, he had to be honest.  People
depended on him.
     He was honest, too, when he promised to
Margery fifty-eight years ago that he would
always love her and stand by her.  They've
been married that long, and now they have
two children and three grandchildren.
     But he was never more honest than the
day, six years ago, when his oldest
daughter's husband, Fred, was in the hos-
pital and Abe went to see him.
     "You need a haircut," said Fred, joking.
     But Abe replied in utter seriousness:
"I won't get a haircut until the day you
walk out of here."
     Fred never did walk out of there.  He
was carried out.  He died.
     And so Abe felt that he owed it to
Fred to keep his word.  That's why he has
never cut his hair, why he has a long white
ponytail--this conservative CPA.
     It is his white badge of honesty,
devotion and love.
```

My Favorite Love Story

On August 27, 1986, I was hired to write 60-Second Novels at a party for CBS Magazines, held at Rye Playland, an old amusement park north of New York City. One of the many people who stood on line for me that day was a pretty blue-eyed woman named Alice, who told me about a recently ended relationship and how she was dealing with it, in part by taking walks along the ocean. In response, I wrote something I almost never do: a prediction for how she would find the man of her dreams.

A Walk Along the Ocean

Alice went out with Jeff for four years and then he broke up with her because he felt it wasn't right and he was confused, which made her very unhappy at the time, but now she thinks it was for the best. In the year and a half or two since then, she has gone out on dates but either she likes the guy and he doesn't like her, or vice versa.

Well, this is all pretty rotten.

So she has taken to seeing her grandmother, a very wise woman, encouraging and loving. Alice talks with her and feels much better, and finds warmth and laughter. But how will she ever find true love?

One day, after visiting her grandmother, Alice will go for a walk along the ocean, and she shall meet a man. He will ask her a question and the first thing she will think is, "Wow, is this guy SOMETHING!" and they will talk and fall in love.

He might come from a ship. He might be swimming. He might be walking. Maybe he will fall from the sky, or maybe he will come from beneath the waves. But the important thing is he will come from the ocean after she goes to see her Grandma and isn't even thinking about a man.

For there are plenty of fish in the sea, and many men, too.

One significant fact I failed to note that day: since Rye Playland is located directly on the ocean's bay, I had been sitting not twenty yards from the shore when I wrote Alice's story. She met me, that is, on the water's edge. Two months later, I walked into a writing class at the New School, a popular adult-ed school in New York, and sat down (by chance? by fate?) next to Alice. We went out for coffee and ended up falling in love.

For all I've learned about love from the thousands of couples I've written for, they didn't teach me peanuts compared to Alice. She was unlike anyone I'd ever dated: exuberant, sweet, thoughtful, honest, tender, funny, smart, talented and beautiful.

On December 23, 1989, I walked her out onto the freezing cold beach in Cape May, New Jersey, and told her to look up at the beautiful stars. When she turned back to face me, I was down on one knee with a Tiffany ring in my hand. "Alice Rose Garbarini, will you marry me?" I asked her.

Thank God, she said yes.

Chapter 4

Department Stories

S oon after writing my way onto the party circuit, I began getting hired by malls, department stores and fragrance companies across America to write stories for ordinary shoppers. One department store in particular—Hess's, which has since gone out of business (not my fault!)—sent me to all their new store openings across the country. At one, cows could literally be seen grazing on the grass surrounding the parking lot. West Virginia coal miners, sixteen-year-old mothers and sixty-year-old grandmas all stood in line to tell me their stories. At an Albany store opening, I met a schizophrenic who literally thought he was Elvis. ("How does it feel to be Elvis?" I asked him. "Elvis's body feels sooo good," he replied.) In Indiana, I met a teenager from Brooklyn who'd been sent out to live with his aunt after being involved in a gang fight that resulted in a man's death.

Usually the stores set me up somewhere in the cosmetics department, and then started making announcements over the public address system: "Shoppers, the 60-Second Novelist is on level one to write your life story." (So much for thinking I was an off-the-wall "performance artist.")

The first couple of times I wrote in the stores, I'd see some ordinary suburban housewife-type, or some disabled person rolling toward me in a wheelchair, and I'd have my presumptions and prejudices. But then the "housewife" or the "disabled person" opened her mouth and suddenly I was listening to an incredible true story about overcoming cancer, or leaving an abusive husband, or having the guts to pursue a crazy romance. And then I'd look at this person before me and wonder: Who would ever suspect?

Ellen Cooperperson

At Bloomingdale's department store in Garden City, Long Island, I was hired one weekday afternoon in May of 1989 to promote an Estée Lauder fragrance. ("Story with purchase.") Things were pretty slow in the store until a woman walked up and I asked her name.

"Ellen Cooperperson," she said.

"Is that your maiden name or your married name?" I asked.

"Neither," she said, and proceeded to tell me the true story of how, in 1976, she had gone to court to have her name legally changed from her ex-husband's name of "Cooperman."

"Why didn't you just go back to your maiden name?" I asked.

"Because my maiden name was my father's name," she said. "I wanted a name that reflected my sense of human equality. It enabled me to make a statement about the sexist nature of our language."

When the judge refused to grant her request, her case was picked up by the media. She appeared on "Good Morning America" and in *People*. Ellen told me more, and then I wrote:

Ellen Cooperperson.

THE MAKING OF ELLEN COOPERPERSON

Ellen was married once, to Mr. Cooperman. It felt like being enslaved or bonded in some way, like being jailed. So she and Mr. Cooperman divorced. She was free of him, but not of his name. In some sense, he had branded her, he had NAMED her, and as they say, it is the powerful who make history, whereas she wanted to make herstory. He had named her as the white men once named the countries of Africa, dividing it into little meaningless pieces having nothing to do with the human beings who lived there. And so Ellen, being a human being and entitled to titling herself, went to a judge and said she wanted to be Ellen Cooperperson.

The judge got tiffed. If she became Ellen Cooperperson, what might happen? Why, manholes might become peopleholes. Africa might return to being hundreds of independent tribes, all free to live their own life, all free to set their own fate. The Third World might be liberated; the poor might go to college; women might do as they please without permission from men; why, the whole world might wake up to name itself, to define itself, to invent itself. And he couldn't let that happen. But Ellen fought his decision, and won the right, and the name.

Alas, the judge's dire predictions did not happen. But Ellen looks to the day when her dreams might yet come true, when we all might finally stop behaving as if we were pinballs in a pinball machine, and awaken to our birthright of life, liberty and the pursuit of happiness--just like Ellen Cooperperson.

My first department store appearance was in Chicago's
Carson Pirie Scott, where I was placed in a window to write
60-Second Father's Day novels.

Just Another Shopper

At a Hess's department store in Syracuse, New York, I learned again the moral of one of Aesop's ancient fables: Appearances can be so very deceiving.

And I Thought She Was Just Shopping

It looks like just another case of a bored housewife with no interest except buying and shopping.
How far from the truth!
Susan was married twice before. First she had a big husband and whenever he got mad, she was the punching bag. He konked out one of her lungs, permanently. This is hard to picture because she is such a cute blonde woman with nice blue eyes.
Then she married a cop to "protect" her. So much for wishful thinking.
Now she is remarried again, this time happily at last. Her husband worked for 10 years for Allied, until he was laid off. Now he works nights at Niagara Mohawk. So Susan works days at Hess's, from 9 to 4, in the electronics department. And then she comes home to this combined family of two children of hers, three of his ███ (and all five theirs). She tries to sort them out, solve the little arguments, and feed them. And then she has nothing else to do. Husband isn't home. And she needs exercise for the remaining lung. She's got to walk. But if she goes outside the kids start running, and she could half-croak chasing them. So the mall here is the only place she can come to, where she can walk and at least look for

things they need, and bring all the kids,
because she doesn't believe in leaving her
kids at home.

So basically, her being at this mall is
a heroic victory against incredible difficulties and challenges, and I think everyone
in the mall should stand up and clap every
time she walks by.

The Survivors

On April 14, 1990, I was writing 60-Second Novels in the Bloomingdale's in Hackensack, New Jersey, when an unusual-looking family walked up. The father had a halo collar around his neck—a metal frame, with a plastic chest brace, keeping his head and neck in place. The two smiling kids, both on the verge of adolescence, wore very thick glasses, and looked much more dark-skinned than their parents. The pretty mom was the only one who looked "normal." I asked what had happened to the dad, and heard their incredible true story.

```
ALETA AND BILL'S JOURNEY


    Aleta and Bill got married and wanted to
have kids. But Bill had been married before,
and Aleta was older. They both had careers,
and both sang in the opera, so they thought
it would be better to adopt. They saw pic-
tures of some children down in the Cran
orphanage in Bogota, Columbia, and decided
to adopt them. Bill went down to pick them
up. They were a brother and xix a sister,
Peter and Bianca, both with congenital
cataracts that made thick glasses necessary.
Peter threw such a tantrum when they left
that Bill decided to take them back for a
final goodbye, even letting Peter hand out
ßxxxtxxkxxkxx candy to his friends. After
that, the kids were ready to go.
    And so on January 25, they boarded
Avianca flight 52 headed for New York's
Kennedy airport. More than an hour past its
```

scheduled 8pm arrival, the plane was still
circling the skies, delayed by weather and
a backup of other flights. Bill already
felt nervous when the plane dipped. He
didn't know that it had run out of fuel,
but as the other passengers began screaming,
and the throb of the engines quieted, he
knew they were about to crash. "God, why
have you done this to us?" he shouted out.
Then he felt the plane hit something, and
he passed out.

A moment later, in dreamlike silence,
he was staring out a hole in the plane,
the wind blowing on his face. He unlocked
the seat belt from his overturned chair and
crawled out the hole, landing face-down in
the mud.

"Peter!" he called out. "Bianca!" But all
he heard was crying and moaning. He wanted
to search for them, but he couldn't move his
head or legs, and even a small movement of
his arm sent a lightning bolt of pain throug
his body.

"This one's dead," he heard someone say.
"This one's alive."

"I'm alive!" Bill shouted to the rescuers.
"Over here!" Floodlights came on, and Bill
saw a hellish scene of luggage, body parts,
seats and clothing strewn across the muddy
ground. A priest appeared and gave Bill his
last rites. Finally he was placed on a heli-
copter, still not knowing if his newly
adopted children were dead or alive.

Aleta waited and waited for him at the
airport with jackets for the children. The
agents told her nothing. Finally they
took her to a hotel. At about 5 o'clock in

the morning, they told her Peter was alive,
the kids were alive, but they had been in
the Avianca crash. Seventy-five people had
died. Eighty-three had lived.

Aleta took a cab to the hospital. On
the way, the cab broke down. She and the
social worker who had been assigned to work
with her had to walk the last mile. Finally
they made it to the hospital, and Aleta
went to her husband's bedside. She squeezed
his hand and told him to squeeze back if he
could hear.

He squeezed. And then she knew that
everything would be all right. Now both the
kids are fine, but Bill is still in a halo
collar.

Yes, a halo from God's blessings.

Chapter 5

The Wisdom of Ordinary People

Sometimes I've felt like an absurd modern twist on Pythagoras, that ancient Greek philosopher who roamed the world in search of wisdom. As the 60-Second Novelist, I can go anywhere to talk to anyone about anything, so I've gone to street corners, nursing homes, private parties and department stores to ask ordinary people for their wisdom. I've ended up learning a lot more from them than I ever learned in four years of college as a philosophy major. Their insights are much messier than the kind I read about in books. It's wisdom lived, not talked about. It's practical and utterly real. How to find happiness. How to accept what cannot be changed.

How to stay married. How to put family ahead of work. The wisdom of the common man and woman, I learned, is pretty cool stuff.

The Perfect Life

On Thursday, December 10, 1998, I was hired to write 60-Second Novels at a Christmas party for Philip Morris in New York City. The whole thing felt like something out of the 1950s. Everyone was drinking martinis, and two beautiful young women—a blonde and a brunette—walked around in skimpy outfits, carrying silver trays with cigarettes on them. Toward the end of the evening, I talked with a woman I'll call Suzanne, a secretary who told me how worried she was that her husband was out of work. He had quit his job as a retail manager at a Pathmark—the same store where she had met him twelve years ago, when she was a cashier. The more she told me about this problem, however, the more I began to think that she was living. . . .

THE PERFECT LIFE

John and Suzanne have been married for
nine years. John was a retail manager at a
Pathmark, working sixty hours a week, never
home, not happy, totally stressed out and
heading for an early heart attack. And then
one day he said to hell with it all and quit.
He's never been happier. He wakes up
singing. Not a joke. He literally wakes up
singing. And not your basic "do-you-know-
the-way-to-San-Jose" songs. He makes up his
own silly songs, in Italian no less. He
thinks they're love songs, but he doesn't
have a clue what he's really saying. He
might as well be singing the virtues of
toilet cleaners, for all he knows. And then
he spends the day doing little chores to
help out, cooking, just feeling happy all
day long.
But Suzanne is worried to death. She
fears for their financial future.
So one day soon, John will find a job
at a Dunkin Donuts or similar establishment,
and he shall dedicate his life to making
people happy, even though he gets paid only
a modest salary. And when he gets home each
night he will still have time enough and
energy enough to sing his silly happy songs
for Suzanne, while making money enough that
she will feel peaceful enough to join in on
the chorus.

Dan Henly

At the opening of a new Hess's department store in Maryland, a woman told me how her mom had once learned this lesson:

Ask God, Don't Tell Him

Gail and Jim lived in a small Southern town in the late 1950s. After five years of a reasonably happy marriage, they still hadn't had a baby. They placed their name on their doctor's adoption waiting list, but he'd explained that hundreds of families were ahead of them--and that very few babies were put up for adoption in their town. They wanted a baby more than anything, but it appeared they would remain forever childless.

Then one spring day, Gail told a friend of her sadness.

"Have you prayed to God?" asked the friend.

"Yes, we've told Him many times how much we want a baby. But God hasn't answered our prayers."

"I have a suggestion," said the friend. "Why don't you try asking God, instead of telling Him."

That night, before they went to bed, Gail wrote in her diary: "Dear God, for years I've been telling You what I want. Now I ask what You want. Is it Your will, Lord, for us to have a baby? If so, we would be thankful."

Spring turned to summer, summer to fall, fall to winter. Late one night, when they were sound asleep, Gail awoke with a start.

"Gail!" someone called out. "Gail!"

Sitting bolt upright in the the dark stillness, she realized it must have been only a dream. She checked the clock, saw that it was 3:19 am, and went back to sleep.

Next morning, the telephone rang. It was the doctor on whose adoption list they'd placed their name.

"You're 259th on my list," he said. "But most of the other families aren't even my personal patients--they just called me because they knew I sometimes arrange adoptions. You live in this town, you're good people. That's why I've decided...I'm going to give you this little girl who was born last night."

"Last night?" said Gail. "What time was she born?"

The doctor checked his paperwork and answered, "At 3:19 in the morning."

It was then Gail remembered the question she'd put to God exactly nine months before --when she asked God for a baby, instead of telling him.

Just another shopper getting her story written at Hess's department store.

Few people manage to lose a great deal of weight—and keep it off. I met one at a party on January 30, 1993, and found out how he did it.

HE LOST 85 POUNDS AND GAINED 109

Jéff had always been overweight, but he was, as they say, "in denial." If someone brought it up, he might never talk to that person again. But then, he didn't feel good about his weight, either.

One day, when he went to Barney's clothing store the summer before his senior year at the Wharton School, the salesman said, "We don't have anything that would fit you."

"Well, can't I try something on?" Jeff asked.

"No," said the salesman.

That did something to him. He'd made fun of his dad for going to the fat man's store, and he wasn't going to no fat man's store now. So he invented his own diet. He didn't need any damn Jenny Craig. He had everything he needed in his own head.

He began eating a 600-calorie-a-day diet. He put his father on it, too. If his mother brought home anything more than he wanted—so much as a head of lettuce—he fined her fifty dollars. Of course, she never paid, but he fined her just the same.

He learned to replace quantity with quality. He became a gourmet's gourmet. He ended up losing 85 pounds.

And then he met Sheri. He fell in love with her beautiful smile. And so he married her, and gained her 109 pounds into his life.

And when the next 8 pounds 12 ounces came along in the beautiful bundle of life named Brett, no scale could weigh Jeff's joy.

On Christmas Eve, 1990, I went with my brother Mike to the nursing home across the street from where he lived in the waterfront town of Belfast, Maine. Mike wore a Santa suit, and I took along my guitar to play Christmas carols—and my typewriter to write a few stories. My favorite of the evening was written for a guy named Ralph, who had lost both his legs to diabetes, but not his appreciation for life.

LIFE IS GOOD

Ralph Wiley was born in 1926, on March 20. There were eight boys and four sisters, yet he says it wasn't a hard life. His father worked in a sawmill in the woods. When Ralph was in fifth grade, the teacher told him to go outside to get a whip, becx because she wanted to whip one of the students.

He walked outside, got the whip and stood in the doorway with it. "If you want it bad enough," he told the teacher, "come and get it, 'cause I ain't coming back in."

That was his last day of school.

Ralph never did marry. He lived with his brother, Cliff. And he worked on a farm, with fifty whiteface cows.

Then he started collecting bottles and cans for the recycling center.

Then his brother died, and Ralph developed diabewtes and lost both legs.

Now he lives here in Bradbury Manor Nursing Home, and he likes it. He rolls around in his wheelchair xx all over the place. He's a happy person who feels like life has been good to him.

Why? After all, so many people would feel diappointed x if they had never married...if they hadn't finished school... if they were old and lost both their legs and were living in a nursing home. Why does Ralph Wiley feel life has been good to him?

"I just do," he says. "I get in bed by myself. I go to the bathroom by myself. I made my bed myself yesterday."

We all make our own beds, and we all have to lie in them. Ralph has made his exceptionally comfortable. Which is why he shall surely rest in peace.

Ralph Wiley and my brother Mike as Santa.

Where the Heart Is

In December of 1990, I went to look for the meaning of Christmas. I had heard stories about homeless people living in shacks on empty lots in Brooklyn's Red Hook neighborhood, and decided to see what Christmas meant to someone living in such a place. I drove past dilapidated three-story apartment buildings, towering projects, bodegas and rubble-strewn lots, but shacks were nowhere to be found. Finally I pulled over to ask a middle-aged man and woman if they knew of any shacks, and they directed me to the corner of Bay and Court Streets. When I pulled up, nothing was there—just an empty lot with a couple of abandoned Dumpsters. I started driving away, when suddenly a black man walked out of one of the Dumpsters, pushing a shopping cart. I jumped out of the car to see who he was.

"My name's Clement," he said. "I live here."

"In this Dumpster?" I asked, incredulous.

He pulled away a blanket that hung over one side of the Dumpster. Inside was a bed, a nightstand, dishes, boxes of stuff—all of it in better order than my own cramped studio apartment.

"But are you happy living like this?" I asked.

His answer became the title of the 60-Second Novel that he permitted me to write for him.

I'M REALLY SATISFIED WITH THE WAY
~~WW~~ I'M LIVING NOW--NOT HAPPY HAPPY
JUST CONTENT

Clement is forty years old and living in
a dumpster.
"It's shelter and I don't feel bad," says
Clement. "It's four walls and a ceiling and a
floor. The only thing it's missing is a
kitchen and a bathroom."
Clement says these last words with an
impish smile. His unlined face seems
younger, except for his graying beard.
Clement has lived here in this dumpster,
in a lot where dumpsters are stored at the
corner of Bay and Court Streets in Brooklyn,
for a year and a half, since breaking up with
his wife and discovering that he really
didn't like the shelters. He's not a drug
addict or an alcoholic. "The only ~~thoust~~
vice I have is cigarettes, and a little
marijuana," he says.
Clement makes his money as a ~~wwww~~
"scrapper." He finds cans, bottles, semi-
precious metals--anything he can turn in for
cash. He also cleans out people's basements
or whatever they want. Amazingly, he earns
up to eight or nine hundred dollars a month,
and saves it in a bank account his sister
keeps for him. He's not on welfare and
won't beg, he says, mostly as a matter of
pride.
"I know I could do a whole lot better,"
Clement says. "But I'm content, the way I'm
living. Not happy happy. Just content."
With Christmas coming up, and the spirit
of miracles and God's grace saving us--all of

us, Christians and Jews and Muslims and non-
believers alike, black and white and every
other race, men and women, Park Avenue
millionaires and welfare recipients in
housing projects--may we all find the
contentment in our own homes that Clement
has found in his.

Dan Hinley

Chapter 6

60-Second Fables

Not everybody who has walked up to me has had a profound lesson to teach or an inspiring story to share. Some were hopeless, some were luckless, some were clueless. Others just happened to have a little problem they hadn't yet solved. My role as a one-on-one storywriter placed me in a unique position. I wasn't there just to report on them; I was supposed to write *for* them. But after the lesson I'd learned at "Taste of Chicago," I was through whacking people over the head with straightforward preaching. Instead, I took a page from Aesop, who hid his instructions for living in deceptively simple, entertaining fables. And so I wrote 60-Second Fables to help them find a way out of their maze, to see things in a new light, to trace a metaphorical path toward the happy ending that had so far eluded them.

At Marketplace Mall in Rochester, New York, I was hired for a few years in a row every Valentine's Day to write love stories for shoppers. In 1991, I met an attractive young woman named Krista who insisted that she was an old maid at the age of twenty-one.

KRISTA THE OLD MAID

Krista never had much of a chance to be young. Her father was a wild character who abused Krista's mom, so they divorced and now he won't have anything to do with Krista. Then Krista's mom remarried, but now she's getting divorced again. Krista herself went out with a guy for two years, but he couldn't handle the commitment and fell out of love and broke up with her in October. Now she's dating two guys but nothing is quite working out, and at twenty-one she already feels old. She thinks that time is running out, that life is passing her by.

So she went to a doctor to regain her youth. "Give me an operation!" she begged. "Make me young again!"

And so the doctor gave her an operation. On her brain.

When Krista awoke from the operation, she shouted, "Thank God Ɪꞩ I'm not married yet! Thank heaven I haven't already gotten saddled with some pathetic macho loser who would treat me as badly as my mother was treated. I have all the time in the world to find the man of my dreams! And in the meanwhile I'm going to have fun and develop myself, learn things, get experiences, see the world, play and work and enjoy."

The doctor liked her attitude so much, he asked her to marry him.

By the time they found him tied up in the broom closet, Krista was halfway to California.

At a department store opening in Clarksville, Indiana, during the last week of February 1989, I met a couple named Margaret and Howard who were hoping to find the spark in their marriage again. And so I wrote . . .

Looking for the Spark

Margaret and Howard had been married 33 years. Howard had been working at the same job for 33 years as well, as an optical foreman. After all that time, they didn't have quite the same spark as they used to. They weren't so young. Their marriage wasn't new and exciting anymore. So they decided to go find the spark that they had lost.

They began by looking in their bed. "Do you see the spark?" asked Howard.

"Turn out the light and maybe we'll see it," said Margaret.

He did, but they didn't. So they went looking in the kitchen. "Do you see any spark in the oven?" asked Margaret.

"That's the pilot light," said Howard.

So they went on a worldwide search. They held news conferences. They put up a photo of their lost spark at the post office, next to the "most wanted" pictures. They placed a description of their lost spark on all the milk cartons in Indiana. They stood in malls with big posters. "Have you seen this spark?" they asked.

Eventually they had to go in search of their lost spark to Japan and Hawaii and

Bermuda and France. They looked at the top of
the Eiffel Tower. They looked in all the
best hotels of the world. They looked on
jets and on cruise boats. And still they
didn't find it.
    In fact, they never would, because
Howard had buried it in kk his basement. He
never wanted to find that damn spark.
    It was way too much fun looking for it.

On January 31, 1991, I wrote stories at a party held by the Exton Mall Retailers Association in Pennsylvania, where a guy named Fred told me that he was hoping to get some peace and quiet after the Christmas rush, so he could collect his thoughts. Here's how I imagined that happening:

```
         FRED COLLECTS HIS THOUGHTS

     Fred's thoughts were scattered. He
didn't know where to find them. Life had
been so hectic, what with managing the
company he works for, that he realized all
his thoughts were had left him completely.
They'd been shot right to hell.
     So Fred hopped in his car and drove out
to the woods. He found a quiet place where
a stream gurgled by and birds chirped. A few
chipmunks played nearby. An occasional leaf
fell to the ground.
     And then, after he had sat quietly for a
long while, he heard it.
     Crunch.
     Ca-runch.
     It was a thought. Slowly creeping up on
him. It approached slowly over the dried
leaves. After an hour it jumped up on his
shoulder and whispered in his ear. The Soon
thoughts Fred heard another coming. And
then another. The thoughts talked to him
and told him all they knew. Then they lined
up in perfect formation formation, row after
row, perfectly ordered. He took out his
shoe box that he had brought for just this
purpose and put each thought in its place.
     At last his thoughts were collected
again. He went home, renewed and
invigorated.
```

At a Caesar's Palace high-rollers party on June 18, 1985, I met a retiree named Angie who complained that she didn't like getting old. The problem, Angie said, was that as she grew up she'd learned "what's what." I decided to rectify her problem with a story.

```
        WHAT'S NOT WHAT


     It's a good thing that Angie was born
old and gets younger and younger the longer
she lives.  Because back when she was old,
she knew all about life and what's what.  But
the longer she's lived, and grown younger
and younger until she's become a little
child, she has gotten a better and better
sense of what's not what.
     She's learned that all those things that
used to annoy her, like laundry and taxes,
are silly and unimportant.  Sometimes, she's
learned, you just have to go out and party,
take a vacation, go on a romantic dinner,
run naked through a fountain, dance to
boogie woogie in the middle of the street.
     And the younger she has become, the
more light-hearted she's become; the more
she values this very moment, rather than
thinking about the past, as she used to  when
she was old.
     But the best thing about slowly growing
into a child is that she now experiences the
simple joy of being alive; she skips and
claps, she sings and laughs over nothing but
the pure pleasure of living.
     Whereas in the beginning, when she was
old, she worried about the laundry and
taxes.
```

At South Street Seaport on October 6, 1984, I met a some-what cynical computer programmer named Nick who said he was against the "system." He seemed to think that everyone in the world was a conformist—except him. I wrote him this story:

UNIVERSE 2.0

Nick was a disgruntled computer pro-grammer in Austin, Texas. He was against the system. He hated all the young urban professionals; he hated everyone conforming. He hated gray suits and gray minds.

So he wrote a computer program that would hook into the fundamental design of the universe itself. And he started rewriting the program that ran the world. His new edition would be known as Universe 2.0.

As a result, instead of most people trying to be cautious and careful, they all tried to be nutty and bold.

Instead of most being gray and conformist, they tried to be only themselves, no matter how idiosyncratic.

Instead of being mindless mall-goers and acquisitive yuppies, they fought for peace and love and understanding.

But there was just one catch. His pro-gram had a bug.

It eliminated Nick's ability to feel superior to everyone.

The release of 2.0 would have to be put off a few more weeks.

Chapter 7

Love at First Sight

Most people question the very idea of love at first sight. "Lust" at first sight, *maybe*, but the love of a lifetime in the blink of an eye? How naive. I certainly didn't believe in it . . . until I met a handful, then dozens, and finally hundreds—literally hundreds—of couples to whom it has happened. In fact, more than one in twenty of the couples I meet tell me they fell in love at first sight. (They seem to run in flocks. At some parties, easily one-fourth of the couples insist, despite my vocal expressions of skepticism, that they fell in love at first sight—and they're eager to tell all about it in convincing detail.) As one who has interviewed more "love at first sight" couples than probably anyone else ever has, I am convinced that not only is the phenomenon real, but that it has something important to teach the rest of us.

Consider: These couples do not merely *feel* instant love; that's the kind of sudden infatuation most every teenager has felt. Rather, the defining element for nearly all couples who truly fell in love at first sight is that within minutes, or maybe hours, of meeting—and yes, sometimes the *moment* they saw each other, whether across a crowded room or when a door opens—they *knew*, although they didn't know how or why they knew, that *this is the person I will marry and be with forever*. It's a kind of knowledge, based on evidence far too paltry for the rational mind to explain.

But there is an explanation. Our rational mind—the one most of us rely on most of the time—is just too dumb to see the Big Picture. Logic is great for breaking things down into tiny little pieces and putting them in cubbyholes. But at sorting through all the myriad, mysterious intangibles that go into the love of a lifetime—or into a career choice, or the writing of a person's life story in 60 seconds—logic is nearly useless.

I doubt that the English poet William Blake was thinking of love at first sight, or, for that matter, about 60-Second Novels, when he wrote these words in 1804, but they apply just the same:

To see a world in a grain of sand
And a heaven in a wild flower,
Hold infinity in the palm of your hand
And eternity in an hour.

What the stories in this chapter demonstrate is the genius of the human mind for literally seeing eternity in an hour or a minute. But *please*—don't think I'm advocating the renunciation of common sense. I've met too many unmarried teen parents to root for *more* impulsive love affairs. What matters most is not how quickly two people fall in love, but how long and strong their love endures.

The Twinge

If love at first sight is going to last, how does a person know? On what basis does someone decide to pursue what could be just a momentary feeling?

At a corporate party in 1989 held by the company that makes Yoo-Hoo, I met a sales executive named Terry Kester, who told me about what he called "the Twinge."

"When I used to place bets on football games," he said, "I always knew I would win when I felt a funny feeling in my stomach—the Twinge. The last time I felt it was on May 19, 1980, when I was returning from a vacation in Jamaica."

As he told his story, I wrote:

THE TWINGE

Terry was on his last day of a vacation in Jamaica with his girlfriend, hoping to patch up their failing romance. But it hadn't worked. He knew they were finished. Then, as they were getting on a bus to the airport, he saw another woman. And when he saw her-- tall, dark, attractive--he felt the Twinge.

On the plane, he found her coming out of the rest room. "We'd make a good couple," he told her. That was his line of the day. But bad weather came up, they both had to take their seats, and he arrived home knowing nothing more than that her name was Barbara and she worked for Pepsi. So he placed an ad in the local paper saying,

BARBARA: Met you on American airlines from Jamaica. Would like to get in touch. Call Terry from Yoo Hoo.

Meanwhile, he had a friend who was able to get him a list of all the Barbaras at Pepsi: 26 in all. He knew she was Italian, so that cut the list in half. He called the first one, and she said, "Are you the one who placed the ad in the paper? I'm not your Barbara, but I wish I was. Everyone in our office is talking about your ad. Good luck! I'll switch you over." He got "his" Barbara on the phone and asked her why she hadn't responded to his ad. "I thought you might be some kind of a nut," she said, and still wouldn't go out with him for a month. But when she finally relented, and opened the door on their first date, Terry knew it was all worth it. Now they've been married eight years and are happy as can be.

Which just goes to show: the Twinge is never wrong!

Ten years later, I contacted Terry and Barbara in preparation for this book. They're still married, with a boy and girl, and Barbara assures me that Terry's still the same romantic nut as the day she met him.

Here's that original personal ad he placed in the newspaper:

BARBARA: From Pepsi Cola-Purchase, N.Y. met you on American Airlines Flight from Jamaica on May 19, would like to hear from ou. Please call Terry Yoo-Hoo

SINGLE? Meet sincere, beautiful people like YOU. Very low fees. Call

At a Manhattan loft party on June 8, 1991, I met a couple named Ilsa and Alan whose story was true, word for word:

THEY MET ON THE 6 TRAIN

Some call it the 6 Train. Ilsa and Alan called it the Love Train. With a name like Ilsa, she could have been in Casablanca, if only Alan would have changed his name to Rick. Had he done that, though, their train would have been in Paris, as the Germans were marching in, and in a cloud of steam and smoke under a dark rain, he would have stood on the steps leading up to the train, waiting for Ilsa, waiting and never finding her, but finding instead only sadness and cynicism.

But his name was Alan, so they met on the 6 Train at 125th Street in Harlem.

The train had two different ꝺꝺꝺꝺꝺꝺ destination signs posted by mistake, so Ilsa asked Alan, this friendly-faced stranger, "Does this train stop at 59th Street?"

Although he knew it didn't, he said, "Yeah, get on," and she did. And as they both entered, he impulsively added, "Having said that, will you marry me?"

"Huh?" said Ilsa, shaking her head. "What did you say?"

ꝺꝺꝺꝺꝺ "Never mind," said Alan sheepishly.

She sat by herself and did some paper-work, thinking her Freudian train-in-a-tunnel thoughts. She found herself remember-ing a scene from the TV show Thirtysomething involving the character named Nancy. In the scene, Nancy's mom meets a man on a train, feels a deep attraction to him--but then just says goodbye. Later, Nancy scolds her mom, "Here you met the man of your dreams, and you never even got his tele- phone number!"

That scene of lost opportunity flashed through Ilsa's mind. She knew it was now or never. So when the train rose up above the ground, into the sunlight, she walked over to Alan and said, "I've been reading the same line ten times over. When's the wedding?"

It's on September 15, 1991--a year and two months after they met.

Who needs Casablanca? They'll always have the 6 Train. All the romantic movies in the world don't amount to a hill of beans compared to Alan and Ilsa's true love story.

Eight years later, I managed to track them down in preparation for this book. "We read your story at our wedding," Ilsa told me. I asked how they were doing. "It's a long, complicated time later," she said. "We had a boy, who is now five and a half, and then we had twins, a girl and a boy. The second boy was born with major, major challenges. What Alan and I saw in each other that morning on the subway was real, but we certainly didn't just ride happily off into the sunset together. The statistics on couples with children who have special needs is that they don't stay together. We did great with no kids, and then great with one kid. The twins, plus the challenges, have made things extremely difficult." How would their story turn out? "I think we're going to get through it," Ilsa replied, "but not easily." What more could be said of any marriage?

Ilsa, Alan and their three children.

Donna's Dream Lover

At a party in New Jersey on the afternoon of April 4, 1992, I met a woman named Donna who told me the kind of story I never would have believed if I hadn't heard it from her personally—and from others at the party who backed it up. Strangely, her true story contained the same three-word question—"when's the wedding?"—as Ilsa and Alan's. What are the odds?

```
DONNA'S DREAM LOVER

    Donna Silverman attended graduate
school to become a social worker at Washingt
ton U. in St. Louis, kind of desperate for
love, cute though she was. Somehow it just
wasn't all coming together. Maybe she was
too profound and serious, thinking about
human suffering as social workers are wont
to do.
    One day she was hypnotized in a class,
as part of her training. And in this hyp-
notic state, she saw herself sitting on the
edge of a pool. A dark-skinned guy with a
beard swam up to her and said, "I'm the
perfect man for you, and when the time is
right we'll meet."
    Months later, she was over at the apart-
ment of Bonnie, her girlfriend. As Bonnie
crocheted, Donna began idly leafing
through Bonnie's college yearbook from the
University of Rhode Island.
    Suddenly Donna was screaming, "Wooooo,
Bonnie, that's him!" She pointed at a
photograph in the college yearbook, of a
dark-skinned man with a beard named Larry
```

Sternbach. "That's the guy I saw under hypnosis!"

Bonnie encouraged Donna to write to him. Donna did, on January 1, 1980.

"One night this stranger appeared to me in a dream," she wrote. "I didn't think much about it until recently I was looking through a URI yearbook and saw your picture. This will probably sound very foolish to you, but I knew that it was you. What were you doing in my dream?"

A few weeks later, she received a letter back. "Before I confess to any intrusions into your subconscious," Larry wrote, "I'd like to clarify a few things. First of all, what WAS I doing in your dream? Did I pull your screaming body from the railroad tracks seconds before the train came? Or was I the one who tied you up?"

With a flirty sense of humor like that, Donna knew this was the man for her.

They corresponded all that summer as Donna and a few friends took a bicycle trip from St. Louis to Oregon. He would send his letters every week or so to the post office at her next scheduled stop. And as she pedaled, she planned their wedding-- still having never met him.

Finally, when the trip ended in August, she flew back to St. Louis and then began driving to Boston, where she was planning to move with Bonnie. On the way, she stopped in New Jersey to meet Larry at last.

When she saw him in person, he exceeded her expectations. Truly he was the man of her dreams. At last she told him the full story about her hypnotic state, and what he'd said to her in it.

"So," Larry said when she finished the story, "when's the wedding?"

Actually, she had shown up on Friday, August 22, so that they could get married precisely one year later, on Saturday, August 22, 1981. Now they have been married over 10 years, they have three kids, and it's been like a.....dream.

Dan Hurley

Donna and the man of her dreams, Larry, have now been married nearly twenty years.

On June 15, 1985, I was writing at my usual spot on Columbus Avenue when a blond, blue-eyed guy named Bruce and a doe-eyed beauty named Nasrin walked up. The tale they told was so incredible, I wrote them a 240-second novel:

```
          US AGAINST THE WORLD

   Bruce had been traveling the world on a
shoestring when he came to Kabul, Afghani-
stan, in 1978, weeks after the Communist
coup. One day he asked directions from a
group of college girls and found himself
gazing into the eyes of Narx Nasrin--beautiful
brown eyes reflecting back at him in an
utterly sincere, guileless fashion. It lasted
only a moment, but when the girls left,
Bruce remained standing like a statue. It
made no sense, yet ƒƒƒƒ he had fallen in
love. From that day forward he was obsessed.
   He looked for this Nasrin wherever he
went. Whenever he saw her, Bruce followed by
foot, bus or bicycle. Of course it was
hopeless--her Muslim religion forbade all
skakaktkakbb dating. And the new Communist
government forbade all contact with
Americans, so he was double cursed. But one
day, after months of following her, Bruce
caught up to Nasrin on an otherwise
deserted street, and for two minutes they
chatted. He mentioned how much he would like
to meet her family, and she gave him the
telephone number of her home. For weeks he
called every day.
   Finally she invited him to visit on a
Muslim holiday. So dangerous was it for an
```

Afghan family to be seen with an American
that he snuck in through a back door, under
cover of dark. Few in Kabul would have risked
such a visit, but Nasrin's father was a
university professor, trained in Europe, and
a doting parent who found it hard to deny
his beloved children. For most of the evening,
Bruce sat talking with them all. Then, for a
brief few moments, he and Nasrin were left
alone. Bruce struggled to tell Nasrin what
was in his heart, but the words would not
come.

The next day, determined to confess his
feelings, he left a letter at her house.
That night he called. "What did you think of
my letter?" he asked.

"I don't think it's possible because of
our cultures," Nasrin said. "And my father
will never say yes."

"If it's because of my religion, I will
become a Muslim," Bruce blurted out. "If it's
because you'd have to leave your home, I
will stay here. Whatever you say I will do,
so why is it impossible?"

Deeply moved by his words, Nasrin agreed
to meet at his apartment. That night he
gave her a necklace, and a chaste kiss on
the cheek--the first time in her life she
had been kissed by someone outside her family.
Yet as she walked home, she touched her cheek
with her hand, then brought her hand to her
lips.

So began their secret romance, skulking
down alleyways, plotting weeks for one hour
together. They were like Romeo and Juliet,
conspiring against their families and
society. All of Bruce's existence funneled
into this enterprise of anticipating and
arranging each meeting. It was them against
the world.

And then his visa expired. Knowing that
the Communists would never renew it, Bruce
wrote to Nasrin's father and asked permission
to marry. Her father refused. Bruce
accosted him on the street.

"You really shouldn't do this," her father
said. "This is dangerous. Things haven't
changed. Goodbye."

On Bruce's last night before returning
home to America, he told Nasrin, "If you
don't write to me, I will kill myself."

"Why shouldn't I write?" she said. "I
am sure you will be my husband."

"You are making these stories up. It's
impossible."

Nasrin's will to marry him only
strengthened during the two years she studied
to complete her degree. Then she begged her
father to let her, a brother and sister flee
from the Soviet regime with freedom fighters
to Pakistan, and from there to America. Her
father refused, until Nasrin spoke the words
he could not stand to hear: "I shall never
be happy until you let me go."

"If you will be happy," he said with a
heavy heart, "go."

They set off on a journey that might well
have ended in death or prison. Hiding under
blankets in the back of the truck, they
drove across deserts, through rivers, over
mountains. The trip was to take three days,
but it dragged on and on. After more than a
week of freezing temperatures, without any
more food or water, Nasrin could see the
hollow circles in her brother's and sister's
eyes--and the fear of death.

When at last they crossed into Pakistan,
more than a year in a refugee camp still
awaited them before the authorities permitted Nasrin to join an uncle in the

United States. She arrived in the cramped, dark basement apartment in Queens, New York, three full years since she had last seen Bruce.

And then, as if in a dream, they were together again, having a simple inexpensive meal at a Manhattan restaurant. So much time had passed, they felt like strangers. With no one to hide from, the thrill of their secret romance in Afghanistan was gone. Could love survive when it was no longer them against the world?

They went on a second date, and another. Slowly they came to know each other as they never had in Kabul. Their love turned out to be real--and this time based not on romantic obsessions, but on kindness, compassion, and courtesy. And oh, those eyes.

And so Nasrin and Bruce held three marriage ceremonies: first civil, then Muslim, then Christian. As the priest performed the final ceremony in Bruce's parents' home, the tears came to Nasrin's eyes. Not until then, surrounded by his family and friends, did Bruce finally believe that he truly was married to this dark-eyed woman from halfway around the world.

The night I met Bruce and Nasrin turned out to be their first wedding anniversary, when they were out celebrating. They have now been married over fourteen years, have two boys and are still very much in love. But they also still fear for her parents and sisters, now living in Pakistan under Muslim fundamentalist rule. To protect against possible reprisals against them, Nasrin asked that I change her and Bruce's name, which I have gladly done.

On February 7, 1987, I was hired by a Buffalo department store, AM&A's, to write Valentine love stories for customers. I wrote forty-two stories that day, as three local television news crews showed up to tape it for their stations. Two days earlier, on February 7, I had written sixty-four stories in a single day at Hess's in Allentown, Pennsylvania. The very last story of that very long day in Buffalo, an elderly couple, both retired, both very soft-spoken, walked up and told me a tale of old-fashioned true love:

The Photograph

In France in the fall of 1944, while fighting in World War II, Bill McMullen received a copy of his hometown newspaper. Amidst photographs of the high school grads, Bill noticed a girl named Geri, who was new to his small Massachusetts town. "This is a pretty nice-looking gal here," he thought. "I wonder who she is."

The photo did something to him. He cut it out and put it in his wallet. He couldn't explain what it was about Geri, yet he felt her picture helped him survive the war. Her photo gave him something to look forward to when he came home. The crazy truth was, he'd fallen for her without ever meeting her. Even when he was transferred to Belgium and the daughter of a local jeweler fell in love with him, Bill felt in his heart that he was destined for Geri.

A few days after returning home from the war, he met her at last in a pharmacy and introduced himself. That night he called to ask if he could take her to the high school's senior reception.

"I have to ask my mother's permission," she said.

"What a greenhorn," Bill thought, but was
happy when she returned to the phone to say
yes.

When they danced, she fit well in his arms.
Didn't step kox on his toes too much. So he
thought, "Maybe this is it." And when he
softly kissed her goodnight, he knew this
was it.

The next evening, as they sat in the back
seat of their friend George's maxx car while

George drove them home
from another dance,
Bill turned to Geri and
said, "You know, it
seems like I've always
known you."

"It seems like I've
always known you too,"
Geri replied.

"While I was over in
Belgium," Bill went on,
"I was friendly with a
girl whose father was a
diamond merchant. He
thought I was going to
marry his daughter. But
I didn't. I just kept
thinking of your photograph. When I left,
her father gave me two diamonds. I'd like to
give them to you. Would you marry me?"

Without even asking her mother's permission, Geri said yes. Forty-five years
later, she tries to explain why: "Some
things, when you do them at the spur of the
moment, in retrospect they were the right
thing to do. It was illogical but it was
right."

Bill and Geri's story so moved me, I asked for their phone number and later flew up to interview them in their home. It turned out they had never been able to have children—unless you counted their beloved nieces and nephews, and their extensive collection of original Tom Clark "little people" figurines. After I had made a fuss of admiring the figurines, Bill and Geri sent me one called "The Wiz" as a gift that Christmas.

We kept in touch over the years, with cards and occasional phone calls. In December 1997—more than ten years since we'd first met—I sent them a card with a picture of my daughter, Anne. I penned a few words about how things were going, and asked how they were. Early in January, I received this note from Geri's sister:

> *I am sorry to inform you that both William and Geraldine McMullen have passed away. Bill died July 10 of heart failure and Geri July 31 of a brain tumor. It has been a great sadness for the family and friends of them both. We wish God's grace on them and thank you for your friendship to them.*

How strange that they had died within a few weeks of each other. When I finished drying my eyes, I dug out my interview notes. One line Geri had said jumped out: "I kind of think we were together other times. When you're born, you don't remember what happened before. Perhaps in another life we were married." Perhaps, I hoped and prayed, yet another life for these two soul mates was just beginning.

Chapter 8

60 Seconds of Fame

I never sought out celebrities, but I never spurned them either. Whether it was Whoopi Goldberg on a foggy October afternoon at South Street Seaport, presidential advisor Vernon Jordan at a Washington party, or Howard Stern's wife, Alison, at a Long Island bar mitzvah, I've always figured that hey, celebrities are people, too.

Jane Byrne, former mayor of Chicago, reads her novel in 1984.

Tom Brokaw

At New York City's Tavern on the Green restaurant, I was writing novels at a party when I saw NBC News anchorman Tom Brokaw sitting at one of the tables. I went right over, typewriter at the ready, and asked him why he'd become a journalist. "I've always been curious, ever since I was a kid," he said. Then I placed my typewriter on a waiter's stand in the corner, and wrote out his story:

```
         TOM BROKAW'S INSATIABLE CURIOSITY


     Tom Brokaw had an insatiable curiosity.
As a child, he had to know why the sky was
blue. Then, as a journalist, he began asking
probing questions.
     "Is the camera on?"
     "Is my makeup right?"
     And of course the biggest one of all: "Is
Dan Rather getting more than me?"
     So insatiable insatiable was his hunger
for knowledge, that he found out what makes
the Earth turn upon its axis, why fools
fall in love, how high is up, and why the
only unchanging aspect of life is that it
always changes.
     But Tom hoped and prayed that the final
answers would never come, the enigmas never
be solved, so that men and women would
always continue their Sisyphean struggle
upward toward the Great Unknown.
     Otherwise the ratings for the evening
news would go all to hell.
```

Tom laughed and took the story with good humor. It was easy to see that he was no stuffed shirt.

Cristina Ferrare

On Monday, April 21, 1997, I was booked to appear on the Family Channel's *Home and Family* show. Everyone should have the experience just once of pulling up to the gates of Universal Studios in Hollywood, pushing their shades down on their nose and getting waved through by the guard. The sun was shining bright, and I felt totally Hollywood.

My driving directions instructed me to "pass the PSYCHO HOUSE on the left," until eventually I found the yellow Home and Family "house" on a hill. My face powdered, my typewriter ready, I was pointed to the couch on the set and sat down next to my fellow guest, the actress Swoozie Kurtz.

When it was time for my segment, I turned the tables and began interviewing the cohost, Cristina Ferrare.

"So Cristina, you're married?" I asked (knowing full well that she had long ago divorced the famous automotive executive John Delorean).

"Yes, twelve years yesterday."

"It's your anniversary? Excellent. And how did you meet your husband?"

"I met Tony up at ABC when he was running the network. I had to have approval from the head of the network for something I wanted to do on *Good Morning America*."

"What did you think of him?"

"I did not like him very much. I thought he was rather arrogant, rude and pompous."

"Wow!" exclaimed her cohost, Michael Burger.

"So how did you manage to fall in love with a guy who seemed arrogant and pompous?" I asked.

"Well, he didn't like me either. The meeting did not go

well, and needless to say, I'm not on *Good Morning America*. But when I was finally separated, I would see him around town, and there was some odd attraction I had to him. But he ignored me and it really made me mad."

"And then what happened?"

"I met him again at a black-tie party. I was sitting at a table, there's no one at the table because they're all dancing. I'm by myself because now I'm separated. He walks over to me, he has his tuxedo on, his gray hair, and he looks at me and I said, 'Would you care to dance?' And he said, 'No,' and walked away. So that really made me mad. But then he turned around and said, 'Yes, I would like to dance.' And the minute he put his arm around me, and I could smell his cologne and him, I just went weak at the knees. That was it."

By now it was time for a commercial break. I began typing, and by the time we returned on live national television three minutes later, I read aloud the story I'd written:

```
          HATE AT FIRST SIGHT

     Cristina met Tony and felt something she
had never felt for a man.
     Hate at first sight.
     So she forgot about him. But then one
night she was without a dance partner. And
there was Tony again. She turned to him and
said, "Can I have this dance?"
     And he said, "No."
     But then, thank God, he thought twice.
He took a second look, and this time he said
yes, he would dance with her.
     And that's when hate at first sight...
turned into the love of a lifetime.
```

Cristina's hand went to her heart. "Oh, can I have that? I've got chills. That is so nice. This is great."

Totally Hollywood.

Vanna White

In March of 1987, I was writing 60-Second Novels at the grand opening of a new Hess's department store in Chesterfield, Virginia, when two middle-aged women stepped up. They noticed the display across the aisle of fashion by Vanna White, and confessed that Vanna was their obsession in life. They loved her so much that when Vanna and Pat Sajak took a whistle-stop tour of the South, Cathy and Lynn drove hundreds of miles to see them. "That was the best day of my life," Lynn said.

I remembered them six years later, when I met Vanna at an Anaheim trade show for the cable industry, where we were both working booths. During a break, I went over and asked Vanna if I could write her a 60-Second Novel. She said sure, and after a brief interview I wrote the following:

THE GUY WHO FOUND JUST THE ORDINARY SMALL-TOWN GIRL INSIDE VANNA

Vanna White had come from an ordinary small town. She was an ordinary small-town girl. And then something extraordinary happened to her.

The wheel of fortune made her a star.

Sometimes it was odd. Old high-school friends she'd grown up with would see her and ask for her autograph, and she thought that was odd as heck. She wanted to be treated just like an ordinary person. She didn't believe her own P.R.

And then ten years ago, she met George at the home of a friend. George was not dazzled by anything other than her own true personality. He didn't ask for her autograph, until he asked her to sign their wedding license. Because he respected her. He was and is a kind man, an understanding man who knows she has to put on those glamorous outfits and dazzle the world. But when she comes home, he makes her feel like just plain ordinary Vanna again.

And when they have their baby, who they expect soon, Vanna will be proud to put her autograph on his birth certificate.

Dan Hanley

Jules Feiffer

The cartoonist/author/playwright Jules Feiffer attended a birthday party in 1988 on Manhattan's Upper West Side, where I was hired to write 60-Second Novels. The moment I approached to write his story, Jules blurted out a tale of woe about a terrible leak in his roof, which was so bad that he and his wife had to sleep in their dining room, and their daughter was sleeping in the maid's room. Here's what I wrote him in response.

The Reclamation

Jules's bedroom began to leak. The roof was falling in.
He and his wife, Jenny, didn't like this. So they moved into the dining room. Halley, their daughter, woke up in a typhoon, so she moved into the maid's room. They had to put garbage cans throughout the apartment to catch the rain. But the rain kept coming, for thirty days and thirty nights.
When at last it stopped, grass had already begun to grow on their carpet.
Jules went off to write cartoons, and when he came back, a maple was growing out of his bed.
His wife, a reporter, returned from covering the Bess Meyerson trial, and found shrubs growing out of their bureau.
A rabbit hopped through the undergrowth. Butterflies flew, dogs barked, cattle roamed, the buffalo returned and then the dinosaurs.

Their bedroom had been reclaimed by nature, and finally Jules threw off his anger and disgust with his landlord, and threw off his clothes, and he and Jenny became Adam and Eve, and they danced merrily in their Edenic bedroom.

It was only then that the landlord finally had the leak fixed.

Just when it was getting fun.

Dan Hurley

Jules grabbed the back of one of my 60-Second Novel jackets and drew what he titled, "A dance to Dan. A 30-second dancer for a 60-Second Novelist."

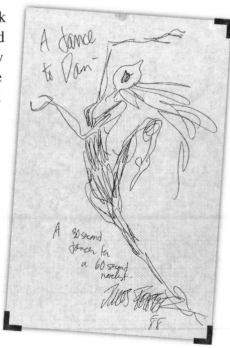

Chapter 9

Twisted Tales by My Evil Twin

Every once in a while I get the devilish desire to let loose with something really weird and twisted. (Imagine Stephen King wandering around your uncle's wedding, writing 60-Second Novels for the horrified guests: "And then out of the wedding cake came a blood-drenched claw. . . .")

But because I hand what I write directly to the person about whom it's written, I've got to watch my step.

Sometimes, though, my evil twin takes over. . . .

My first summer of writing 60-Second Novels in Chicago, most of my stories were off-the-wall inventions, written in direct response to whatever people said and did around me. If two college-age kids walked up and said, "Write a story about fly-by-night monkeys"—as happened late one Friday night on Michigan Avenue in August of 1983—I instantly began typing away:

Fly-By-Night Monkeys

I was living in Uruguay, trying to write novels alone in a cabin, so that no one would disturb me. And yet I was constantly disturbed by these strange visitors. They were fly-by-night monkeys. By day they would walk. But by night they would fly into my windows and sit at my fireplace. They ate my chocolate cake and drank my hot cocoa. They slept with my wife and brushed their teeth with my toothbrush. They kicked me out of bed and ripped up my manuscripts. Those darn fly-by-night monkeys, what a bother! And in the morning, they were gone, and everything returned to its place. My wife didn't even remember.

"But they were here!" I would tell her. "They were here, those fly-by-night monkeys."

At last, watching them fold the pages of my novel into paper airplanes, I hatched a plan to get rid of them. As they were leaving that night, I called out, "Please, take me with you!"

They grabbed me by the arms and flew me to their secret island a hundred miles off the coast, hidden in a permanent fog, without telephones or electricity or any man-made conveniences. We drank banana wine and played cards until they passed out. Then I quietly pulled out my scissors, and methodically clipped all their wings. "The fly-by-night monkeys shall fly no more!" I cackled.

Not until an hour later, when I had carefully searched the entire island, did I discover one small problem.

No boats.

Dan Hurley

READER/CUSTOMER CARE SURVEY

If you are enjoying this book, please help us serve you better and meet your changing needs by taking a few minutes to complete this survey. Please fold it and drop it in the mail.

As a special **"Thank You"** we'll send you news about new books and a valuable **Gift Certificate!**

PLEASE PRINT   C8C

NAME:_____

ADDRESS: _____

_____

TELEPHONE NUMBER: _____

FAX NUMBER: _____

E-MAIL: _____

WEBSITE: _____

(1) Gender: 1)_____Female 2)_____Male

(2) Age:
1)_____12 or under   5)_____30-39
2)_____13-15   6)_____40-49
3)_____16-19   7)_____50-59
4)_____20-29   8)_____60+

(3) Your Children's Age(s):
Check all that apply.
1)_____6 or Under   3)_____11-14
2)_____7-10   4)_____15-18

(7) Marital Status:
1)_____Married
2)_____Single
3)_____Divorced/Wid.

(8) Was this book
1)_____Purchased for yourself?
2)_____Received as a gift?

(9) How many books do you read a month?
1)_____1   3)_____3
2)_____2   4)_____4+

(10) How did you find out about this book?
Please check ONE.
1)_____Personal Recommendation
2)_____Store Display
3)_____TV/Radio Program
4)_____Bestseller List
5)_____Website
6)_____Advertisement/Article or Book Review
7)_____Catalog or mailing
8)_____Other_____

(11) What FIVE subject areas do you enjoy reading about most?
Rank: 1 (favorite) through 5 (least favorite)
A)_____ Self Development
B)_____ New Age/Alternative Healing
C)_____ Storytelling
D)_____ Spirituality/Inspiration
E)_____ Family and Relationships
F)_____ Health and Nutrition
G)_____ Recovery
H)_____ Business/Professional
I) _____ Entertainment
J) _____ Teen Issues
K)_____ Pets

(16) Where do you purchase most of your books?
Check the top TWO locations.
A)_____ General Bookstore
B)_____ Religious Bookstore
C)_____ Warehouse/Price Club
D)_____ Discount or Other Retail Store
E)_____ Website
F)_____ Book Club/Mail Order

(18) Did you enjoy the stories in this book?
1)_____Almost All
2)_____Few
3)_____Some

(19) What type of magazine do you SUBSCRIBE to?
Check up to FIVE subscription categories.
A)_____ General Inspiration
B)_____ Religious/Devotional
C)_____ Business/Professional
D)_____ World News/Current Events
E)_____ Entertainment
F)_____ Homemaking, Cooking, Crafts
G)_____ Women's Issues
H)_____ Other (please specify) _____

(24) Please indicate your income level
1)_____Student/Retired-fixed income
2)_____Under $25,000
3)_____$25,000-$50,000
4)_____$50,001-$75,000
5)_____$75,001-$100,000
6)_____Over $100,000

TAPE HERE DO NOT STAPLE

||||||

BUSINESS REPLY MAIL
FIRST-CLASS MAIL PERMIT NO 45 DEERFIELD BEACH, FL

POSTAGE WILL BE PAID BY ADDRESSEE

HEALTH COMMUNICATIONS, INC.
3201 SW 15TH STREET
DEERFIELD BEACH FL 33442-9875

|.ll...ll..l..l.l..l..l.ll.l..l..l.l...l.l.l..l.l.l

FOLD HERE

((25) Do you attend seminars?
1)_____Yes   2)_____No
(26) If you answered yes, what type?
Check all that apply.
   1)_____Business/Financial
   2)_____Motivational
   3)_____Religious/Spiritual
   4)_____Job-related
   5)_____Family/Relationship issues
(31) Are you:
1) A Parent?_____
2) A Grandparent?_____

Additional comments you would like to make:

_____
_____
_____
_____

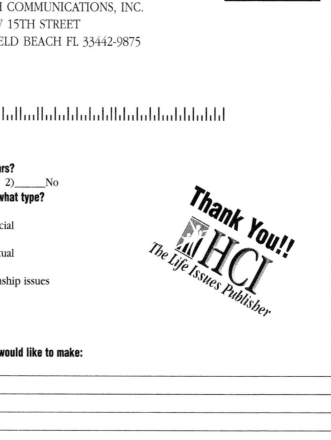

N-CS   C8C

A woman walked up to me on Columbus Avenue one afternoon and told me how frustrated she was by her experiences
in a small town in Massachusetts, where a local hunter had
killed her beloved dog. I wrote this Twilight Zoney story to
give her a sense of getting even.

MURDOCH'S ~~RETURN~~
REVENGE

Two years ago, Jayne lived in a small town
in Massachusetts. At that time, her Great
Dane, Murdoch, was first shot, then run over,
by a local hunter. Jayne was quite upset by
this. She loved her dog, and resented the
redneck town and how they seemed to dislike
her and her red Caddilac convertible.

So finally she knew she had to return, to
see that hunter and have it out, once and
for all. Jayne wanted revenge.

She rented another red Caddy convertible,
and drove up by herself. When she reached
town, she headed over to the man's house, a
rustic affair deep in the woods. Outside
she heard nothing but the rustling of tiny
birds in the leaves.

She knocked at the door, but no one
answered. "Hello?" she shouted.

Suddenly she heard a reply from within:
"Who the hell is it?"

"It's me, Jayne. I want to talk to you
about my dog, Murdoch. Didn't you kill him?"

From behind the door the voice replied,
"I did not have anything to do with your
dog's death. I question whether your dog
ever died, in fact."

"Don't be a stupid redneck," she yelled, beside herself. "You know damn well you ran my dog over."

"Ma'am, I'm afraid I'll have to ask you to leave now," came the voice. "The last thing I want to say is: Your dog is much better off now than he ever was with you."

"That's it!" Jayne shouted. She felt an irresistible need to confront the man, face to face, to grab him and dig her nails into his flesh. And so she walked around the side of the house, saw an open window, and climbed in. She saw him sitting there, his back to her, facing a fireplace. Without thinking, she picked up a vase to crash over his head. A few more steps and she stood before him.

"My God!" she gasped, letting the vase fall to the floor.

Sitting in the chair was her dog, Murdoch, dressed in a man's clothing. And on the mantelpiece was hung the head of the hunter.

"I told you," said Murdoch, "that I'm much better off than I had ever been before."

Dan Hurley

At the convention of the National Association of College Activity Planners, in February of 1988, a woman named Rita told me that she divorced her ex-husband because he'd turned into a couch potato. I took her literally.

THE POTATO BLIGHT

Rita was married for twelve years. She had married a man, but she divorced a potato.
When they started they were good friends, both from a rural area of West Virginia. Rita was the tenth of eleven children. She enjoyed Jim's friendship, so she married him. But as she started pursuing adventures like climbing mountains and jumping out of airplanes, Jim merely progressed from watching "Leave It To Beaver" to watching "All in the Family."
Eventually, he turned into a potato.
First his legs fell off. Then his hair fell out. His nose dropped. Finally all that was left was his rounded body and his eyes and his mouth to put food and Coke in.
And so Rita filled him with butter and sour cream and served him to another woman. She was a woman who loved spuds, and she married him as soon as Rita had divorced him. And so Rita continued jumping out of airplanes and climbing mountains with a man named Steve who still has legs.
God save him from the potato blight.

Dan Hurley

At a corporate family day on June 25, 1997, a young teenage boy told me that he wanted to be an ophthalmologist. "Why?" I asked him. "I like eyes," he replied. Suddenly a demented little story formed itself in my mind:

"I LIKE EYES," HE SAID

Finally the police broke into Peter's house. He lived in a big old broken-down mansion on the top of a hill, surrounded by thorn bushes and vines and weird snakes and wild animals.

The police broke down the door and saw them.

The bottles, on every shelf in the house, lining every wall.

The bottles with something in them.

Eyes.

They were all filled with eyeballs.

"Oh my God, how could you?" the police asked.

And Peter, with his ragged beard, his torn clothing, his stench from never bathing, his bad breath and his rotting teeth, explained it all with three words: "I like eyes."

On September 5, 1985, on Columbus Avenue in New York, a young professional violinist named Maria told me how her stage fright made her unable to play as well in front of people as she could while practicing alone. I wrote her the perfect solution:

MARIA'S FINGERS

Maria played the violin. She was quite gifted. As a child, she was accepted intò the prestigious Juilliard prep school. She played like a bat out of hell.

Then came adolescence and acne. She developed severe self-consciousness and shyness. Her hands began to shake with nervousness. Every time she went to perform, she felt as though she were standing naked before the audience, that everyone x could see her acne, and that they would laugh. She knew her thoughts were irrational, but she could not stop them. She knew she could be great, x in her fingers, but unfortunately her fingers were connected to her brain.

Until one evening, when Maria fell asleep after dinner, her fingers crawled off her hand and down the stairs to the street below. Her fingers hailed a cab and went to Carnegie Hall. Her fingers got up on stage and played the greatest violin solo ever. The next morning The New York Times hailed them as the greatest violin fingers in the world.

By then they had reattached themselves to Maria's hands. "I should have given you freedom from my brain long ago," she told her fingers, petting them against her cheek.

And from then on, she let her fingers do the walking. And the playing.

At a bar mitzvah on March 25, 1989, I saw a woman clutching her nine-month-old baby at one of the tables.

"Why did you bring your infant?" I asked, perplexed.

"Robby would have been very upset if I hadn't," the mother replied.

"Who's Robby?"

"The baby."

Unable to resist, I wrote the following:

```
        Robby's Traumatic Experience


   Robby was sitting in his shrink's
office. He was an overweight
accountant--sweating, balding,
smoking cigarettes nonstop. He was
divorced. He was being sued by half
his clients.
   "So, Robby," said the psychiatrist.
"Tell me about your early years."
   "Well, doc," said Robby, "you see,
it all started when I was nine months
old. There I was, this helpless
little guy with these incredibly cute
blue eyes. I was teething. And I was
nursing at my mother's breast. And
then, one night, my whole world was
turned upside down. They said it was
a bar mitzvah. They tried to explain,
but how was I to understand? I was a
kid! And there they left me with a
stranger. With bottled milk! With
no one to soothe my aching teeth! I
screamed, I cried, I couldn't sleep,
and then--"
   The psychiatrist shook his arm.
```

"It's okay, Robby, it's okay," said
the psychiatrist, still shaking his
arm, shaking and shaking until
suddenly Robby opened his eyes and
realized it was all a dream. His
beautiful wife, Fiona, was waking
him up. He was the head of a major
corporation. He was young, fit,
happy, healthy.
    "Thank God," he said to Fiona,
"that my Mom took me to Bradley
Steinfeld's bar mitzvah!"

Bid Day

One of the weirdest stories I ever wrote was a true one, for the *New York Times*. It was based on what I witnessed when I flew to Fort Worth, Texas, for two days of writing 60-Second Novels at Texas Christian University in August of 1988. As it turned out, I had arrived on Bid Day, when the college's sororities send "bids," or invitations, to those female students they'd like to have join their sorority. This was the culmination of Rush Week, when the Greek societies threw big parties to figure out which students might be suitable. The invitations were scheduled to appear in students' mailboxes at 5:30 P.M., and all afternoon, as I wrote in the blazing Texas heat in front of the Brown Upton Student Center, they talked about little else.

One young woman told me she had committed "suicide" by choosing only one sorority to be rushed by; if that sorority didn't offer her a bid, she would presumably be left out in the cold and rain to die of social ostracism. Another worried that she was too serious for the sororities, that she wasn't wild and crazy enough.

Still another, Loralee, told me how difficult it was "to find one that's really 'me.'" For her, I wrote the following story:

The Loralee Sorority

Loralee was waiting to find out if she would be accepted to the sorority of her choice. She wanted to go to one that was really HER.

Everyone in her sorority would have red hair.

Everyone would chew gum and have blue eyes and freckles.

Everyone would swim and read a lot of books.

Everyone would have a boyfriend for two years in high school. They would all be outgoing and friendly. And they would all love Danielle Steele.

Finally Loralee found that of course she had been accepted into the perfect sorority for her. It was called the Loralee Sorority. Unfortunately, no one else had been accepted. And no one ever would. It was her very own private sorority of one.

Because no one else could ever be Loralee.

Dan Hurley

I finished for the day at five o'clock, and then stood by with notebook in hand to watch the Bid Day festivities.

At precisely 5:30 P.M., nearly 500 of the women students received bids in their mailboxes inside the student center. Then, as a trumpet played "charge" beneath a cloudless Texas sky, they burst out the front doors into the 103-degree heat, yelling, skipping, laughing, hugging and crying. "We're sisters!" shrieked one young woman, running into the open arms of a new member named Tiffany. All the future sorority sisters dashed a quarter-mile across campus to face a double row of about two hundred young men—literally a gantlet—between whom the girls were supposed to run while the guys, bound by tradition, grabbed them anywhere and everywhere. As I watched, some of the men stood back politely and let the women go squealing by with no more than an obligatory howl, while others bunched up to stop the girls in their tracks, then reached out and touched someone.

I was so amazed that I called the national desk of the *New York Times* and offered to write a piece. I had written a few freelance articles for the *Times*, and thought this might make a great one. The editor I reached gave me the go-ahead, and two hours later I was calling in my article, word for word, comma for comma. My report on TCU's Bid Day appeared on page A16 of the August 25, 1988, edition.

I later heard that they canceled their traditional Bid Day celebrations the next year. That put them a decade ahead of Princeton University, which announced that it would cancel its Nude Olympics, the traditional naked midnight run following the year's first snowfall, after the 1999 festivities resulted in public lovemaking, molestation, and five students hospitalized for alcohol poisoning.

Chapter 10

60 Seconds in the Life of America

B y the summer of 1990, I'd written over 11,000 stories and was beginning to feel somehow tainted by success. Sixty-Second Novels had become a job.

Back in the summer of 1983, I'd actually made fun of just such a possibility when a reporter for the Chicago *Sun-Times* walked up and asked me, "What are you doing?"

WHAT AM I DOING?

I like to watch the people go by and look at me, having no idea what in the world I'm doing. I especially savor those scrunched noses of women who seem almost angry at me; the businessmen who walk by and wave their hand "no" at me from behind; the people who laugh and say "great idea" and keep walking; and the ones who absolutely ignore me, as if I didn't exist.

Now that I'm being interviewed by the Sun-Times, I fear that people might begin to understand me. This might become a business. It might turn into a profession.

And then I'd be arrested for not having the right diplomas.

Now I could see that what I'd made fun of seven years earlier had come to pass: I was trapped by the very thing that had originally freed me from the predictable, tedious toil of the American Bar Association. I was on my way to becoming a hack, a two-bit mall entertainer, and 60-Second Novels would be reduced in the end to a mere gimmick. I was ready to quit.

It was then I remembered an idea which, like my original idea for 60-Second Novels, I'd dismissed as absurd and impractical. The idea centered around an image: I would be in the middle of an Iowa cornfield, dressed in my seersucker suit and bow tie, with my type-writer in my lap. I would be sitting there waiting for someone to walk by, and when he or she saw me I would calmly say, "Hello, I am here to write your life story," and the person would think I was a hallucination or a visitor from Mars. Or I would be out in the desert somewhere, with no fences around, tumbleweeds blowing past, and I would be typing,  typing, typing in the wind: a kind of modern-day Ezekiel. I would travel across the country to write for cowboys in Texas, for ranchers in Wyoming, for lobstermen in Maine, to find America, to get the heck out of New York, and maybe to give one final hurrah to the 60-Second Novel.

My response to this idea for the past two years had been, "Nyaaaaah! That's nuts!" But late one evening in June, after returning from my last bar mitzvah of the spring season, I casually flipped open my calendar. Blank. It was gloriously blank from the end of July through the middle of September. Suddenly the thought of spending that hot month and a half wedged inside my shoe-box apartment seemed a lot nuttier than jumping in my car and taking off across America.

Inconvenience Store

Heading north a month later on coastal Route 1 toward San Francisco, I pulled into the driveway of a Stop N Go in Ventura around 10:00 P.M. Inside, one of the women behind the counter looked to be about eleven years old. "You're pretty young to be up this late," I said to her with a smile.

"I'm just helping out my mom," she said.

Mom looked over and said, "This is the only time I get to spend with her."

Now here was a story waiting to be told, of working too hard in America, going too fast and serving too many.

I told the mom I was a writer, and asked if I could write her a 60-Second Novel. She couldn't have looked more excited if I'd been Jay Leno asking if I could bring her on the *Tonight Show*. Here's what I wrote them:

It's a Convenience Store for Everyone But Gayle

Tonight it's Sunday at 10 pm, and Gayle at least knows where her daughter, Candy, is. She's right here at the Stop N Go with Gayle, where Gayle works her second job.

During weekdays, she's a school bus driver for handicapped kids here in Ventura. And then usually she works another 20 or 30 hours a week here at the Stop N Go. "But this week I worked over 45 hours here. So I worked 71 hours in all."

Why so many hours? "Because I'm a single parent."

There's a lotta bills being a single parent. "Lotta clothes," says Candy, who's wearing a Bart Simpson T-shirt.

Once or twice a week, Gayle brings Candy with her to the store, "just to spend some time with her."

"Cause I'm bored," says Candy.

"No, cause I love you," says Gayle.

Candy feels good about her mother working so hard. "She needs to support me or else we wouldn't have six birds and two cats."

People like Gayle deserve an award for working so hard and being such a good mom under such trying circumstances. As a representative of the people, I commend her rare devotion.

Dan Hurley

I jumped back into the car and a few days later had made it to San Francisco, where I wrote for a couple of days at the famous Pier 39. One windy afternoon, I was approached by a man named Robert, who told me:

THE BRAIN IS A POWERFUL ORGAN

Up rolls Robert in his wheelchair. Seven and a half years ago, at the age of 21, he returned home from college and got into an accident, injuring his spinal cord. But he is absolutely undiminished by this accident. He's handsome, smiling, handsom charming.

Today Robert is with his beautiful wife, Shelley. She has this wonderful crazy jacket with all kinds of spangles and shiny buttons, swirls and curlicues.

"I wanted to marry him the first night I met him," says Shelley. "He was unlike any other man I ever met. His energy. He had such a will to live."

Four weeks after they met, Robert asked her to marry him. There he was in a wheel chair, and this beautiful, vivacious woman said "yes."

Now they've been married just over a year. And on Valentine's Day, 1990, little Shauna was born.

Less than 1 percent of spinal-cord-injured men remain potent and able to have children, they explain. But somehow Robert retained his capability. How'd he do it???

"The brain is a powerful organ," Robert answers. "People don't realize the power of the brain. It's unlimited. It's able to compensate for people's limitations. If you want to be happy, you can be happy."

Robert, Shelley and Shauna are living, powerful proof of that.

Eureka

Three days later I woke up in Winnemucca, Nevada, and headed north on Route 95 toward Boise. To get there, I had to drive through a section of southeastern Oregon unique on all the maps of the states I'd been through so far, because virtually nothing was listed there: no sights, no towns, no points of interest. I soon found out why. The highway went so straight, the cars traveling on it were so few, that I actually started reading the paper while driving eighty miles per hour. A storm came up so strong that I nearly lost all visibility and pulled over to the side of the road. Twenty minutes later, the sun was out, the sky blue.

Without realizing it, I had wandered into the very section of the country I'd had in mind when I first envisioned the journey: the sagebrush desert. With nothing to look at, no traffic to worry about, nobody to talk to and not even any radio stations to play, my spirit was touched for possibly the first time in my life by something that had become incredibly rare in America by the last decade of the twentieth century: *nothing*. Until now, my trip across the country had been marked by too much of everything. There had been too much corn in Indiana. Too much land to drive across in New Mexico. Too many tourists in the Grand Canyon. Too much food and money in Vegas. Too many people in California, too many convenience stores and too much development.

But here, alone in the midst of nowhere, I found my refuge from the masses. Only now, after searching for America across 4,000 miles of highway and side road, could I at last say I'd found it, at last say "eureka." And so I wrote:

EUREKA

Driving along Rt. 95 North toward Boise,
I saw open range land--no fences, no people,
no houses, no cars. The clouds so close I
could have gotten on a step ladder and
touched them. Twisted pale green sagebrush
covering the wet muddy soil, and foamy-light
rocks, as though from the moon. Quiet like
music, wind playing my ear like a flute.
I stopped the car and got out, walked into
it all and thanked God. It took me deeper
than the Grand Canyon, higher than the
Rockies, wider than the Pacific, more fertile
than Indiana. For I was alone with America,
alone with our country, our land.
I drove on then, blasting Billy Joel on
the tape player. But I had to turn around.
I had to write a story for America, a novel
out here alone with the sagebrush. And so I
started to cry, driving back to the open
country, realizing how much I love this land,
this continent. But then suddenly I noticed
my gas level indicator hovering near empty,
and I couldn't drive all the way back to the
spot where I'd walked. And so I stopped
here, at a site explaining the reclamation
project begun in 1962, the Vale Project, to
reseed and restore the rangeland. I walked
out to the edge where a barbed wire fence
held me in. I thought, I shouldn't do it
here, I need to get beyond fences. And
then I crawled under it. My I lifted my
typewriter, my chair, my paper and carbons.
And now here I find myself not alone. I
find America here in the middle of Idaho,
vast and awesome. I sit with you, America,
and with God. So glad I found you at last.

After I finished typing the story (including the mistaken line about being in Idaho, when in fact I was still about ten miles west of it), I snapped a photo of the paper in my typewriter, with the sagebrush and heavy clouds beyond. I kept looking, looking out at the desert. For a few miraculous moments, my mind's eye was able to leap over the horizon, to round the curve of the earth and see as one, in a single instant, the entire country. It was this experience of America being present to me, of standing face to face  with her, which so overtook me that I began to cry. And in this moment of union and connection, I knew—don't ask me how but I just knew—for the first time in my life that there is a personal God, a mother and a father to us all who connects us to each other and to something greater than ourselves, who could indeed be bothered with little Dan Hurley, a God who isn't some distant executive of a far-flung multi-galaxy corporation, but a presence as close as my heart. God's finger touched my soul that day as strongly as my own fingers had touched the keys of my Remington.

And so I folded up my chair, returned the typewriter to its case, crawled under the barbed-wire fence and walked weak-kneed back to my car. When I saw again the gas-level indicator pointing to empty, I no longer worried about running out. Whatever happened now, whether I ran out of gas in the middle of the desert or crashed the car or got thrown in jail, it was all fine with me, because it was all the same country, and there was no longer any wrong place to be in it. A deep sense of peace and safety came over me, then, which lasted the rest of the trip. The journey wasn't mine to screw up anymore. And so my deepest experience of "eureka," besides the discovery of my God and my country, was the discovery of my faith.

Iowa Hog House

Driving north from Des Moines on Sunday, August 25, I saw a tiny sign on the highway for the United Church of Christ in Alleman. I took the turn and walked into the church at 10:00 A.M. Two minutes after I sat down in a pew, the service was over.

"Are you coming to coffee?" asked a sixtyish woman who'd been sitting next to me. "We always love to meet new people."

I thanked her for the invitation and said I'd be delighted to join them. By the time I reached the table of coffee and donuts in the basement, ten more people had introduced themselves. Before I knew it, they'd gotten out of me why I was traveling across America.

"Everybody, I've got an announcement to make!" boomed the minister, Bob Tripp, as soon as he'd met me. All of the fifty or so gabbing people happily quieted down. "We've got a special guest here today, Dan Hurley, from Brooklyn. He's a writer, and I'm sure you'll all want to give him a nice hello!"

Instantly I was surrounded by people shaking my hand and welcoming me. They all seemed so interested in my 60-Second Novels that I asked if I should get my typewriter from the car. Definitely, they said. Five minutes later, I was typing away with what looked like half the congregation watching.

Three of them ended up insisting that I follow them to lunch at the nearby Jade Garden: Frieda and Dean Lehman and their widowed sister-in-law, Selva. I was a little surprised that Iowa farmers would have a Chinese restaurant to eat at, and they admitted that things had changed a great deal from the old-fashioned days.

"I can remember when going out to a restaurant was a big deal," said Frieda, as we settled into our chairs.

"People didn't go out to dinner too often back then?" I asked.

"Well, in those days, we didn't call it dinner," said Dean. "We called dinner supper. And what we called dinner was lunch."

"And lunch was in-between," said Frieda. "It was just a snack."

"So dinner was supper and supper was lunch?" I asked, totally confused.

"No, dinner was lunch," said Dean, "supper was dinner, and lunch was in-between."

It was beginning to sound like the Abbott and Costello "Who's on first?" routine, so I let it rest. But they told me about so many other, more significant changes on the farm as we sipped our egg-drop soup. Their son, Kurt, now farmed the same area of land that seven families used to farm; it had become that much more mechanized. Few of the remaining farmers had the cows and pigs and chickens that all the local families once had. Unless they were doing it as a serious business, animals were an expense they could no longer afford. In fact most of the families living nearby weren't even farmers anymore; they worked in Des Moines and commuted. None of them were likely to be in a card club for thirty-five years, as Frieda and Dean had been. It seemed they were the last of a breed, that the classic American farmers' way of life was vanishing before my eyes.

When the bill came, they insisted on paying it. Then Dean and Frieda took me over to see the huge farm run by Kurt. He wasn't home, but his wife, Lynda, was. She asked if I'd like to see the hog house, and before I knew it they were giving me big rubber boots and overalls to put on. Lynda took me into the farrowing house, where the female hogs give birth, and let me hold a baby pig. When I put it down, the cute little critter nearly peed on my typewriter. I couldn't bring myself to tell them I was a vegetarian, but I did ask Lynda a lot of questions about how the hogs liked it here. When she told me about one hog who hated it so much that she finally escaped, I knew I had to write that hog's story:

ESCAPE FROM THE FARROWING HOUSE

Lynda and Kurt have about four hundred fat hogs on their farm here in Alleman, Iowa. They sell about a thousand head a year. But they're all individuals.

This one gilt--a female who's never had a baby before, but who was pregnant--was feeling unhappy in the farrowing house.

"I think she was claustrophobic," says Lynda. "Kurt would say I'm crazy. But she kept rolling over, sitting up, couldn't get comfortable, huffing and puffing."

It's not hard to see why a hog would get nervous. It's kind of tight in there. Lynda and Kurt don't have the room to let the hogs run around outside, plus if they did go out-side and had babies, they might sit on the babies, or the babies might get in the mud and get hurt. So it's just necessary to keep them inside here. It's not bad conditions in some ways--75 degrees in winter, not so hot in summer. "Probably a lot better than a lot of homeless people have," says Lynda.

But this one hog didn't like it, just the same. Finally, a week ago Saturday, Lynda opened up the door ~~and the crate~~ to let her go outside. She hopped right out when Lynda opened the gate, and stayed out there a few days. Then ~~whe~~ they went away for the weekend, and when Lynda came back, the hog was gone. Free. Outa there. An escaped hog.

She could live out there in the fields the rest of ~~the~~ her life, eating grass, drinking from a pond, keeping warm by a fence row, or burrowing into the ground. Not a good business for Lynda and Kurt.

But it kinda gives a hog hope.

Dan Hurly

Writing in a Cornfield

As I stooped over my typewriter in the farrowing house, writing in my rubber boots and coveralls, I knew I couldn't have found a better experience of Iowa had I searched for sixty years. After chatting a few more minutes and taking some photographs, I got out of the boots and coveralls, thanked them for their hospitality, and drove away through the thick Iowa heat.

By now the temperature was well into the nineties, and I quickly pulled off first my bow tie—which I'd been wearing beneath the coveralls—then my shirt. After driving past miles of corn and beans planted in mathematically precise rows, I found myself remembering one of the original, motivating visions I'd had at the beginning of my trip across America: to type in the middle of an Iowa cornfield. And then I saw a sign for a town named Story City. I had to take the exit. I drove a few blocks to where the cornfields began, waited till no cars were passing, made a dash into the corn rows with my typewriter, and started typing a letter to my brother Mike:

Sunday, Aug. 25, 1990
Inside a cornfield in
Story City, Iowa

Dear Mike:

   I am literally crouching over in the midd
middle of a corn row in a town called Story City.
The wind is blowing, crackling the drying stalks of
the sweet corn. It's about 96 degrees, and I'm x
sweating all over the typewriter. A bug is buzzing
in my ear, insects are rhythmically whizzing, like
the sound a discus thrower might make when he
throws. The earth is black, rich. No weeds. Nothing
but me, dirt, bright sunlight peeping throughin a
few slants, and corn.
   I'm sorry, I feel too ridiculous sitting here
in the cornfield. I keep picturing a farmer
coming to ask what I'm doing.
   Oh to hell with it, I'll keep going. Maybe I'll
get arrested for typing in a cornfield. That would
be perfect.
   So anyway, since I last wrote you, I've been to

I finished typing the one-page letter, and then walked back
to my car, where I took off my sneakers, caked two inches
deep with gooey soil, set them beneath the rear window to
dry, and headed east.

The First Day of Kindergarten

The principal of the Indian Hills Elementary School in Romeo, Michigan, gave me his okay to write 60-Second Novels for some of the kids before their first day of kindergarten began at eight o'clock on a Monday morning near the last day of August.

Romeo is just thirty miles north of Detroit, but its semi-rural roads are a world away. Mothers stood at the ends of their driveways with their two or three children beside them, all of them dressed immaculately and carrying shiny new lunch boxes. Corn grew across the street from the school, a red-brick, one-story building that looked to be from the 1960s—as did the entire town.

I arrived at 7:30, and a few students, parents and teachers were already milling around waiting for the bulk of the children to arrive in school buses. With the permission of her mother, I started out by asking a five-year-old girl named Devin how she was feeling.

"I'm shy," she said.

Yet she looked so well prepared: She had the prettiest blonde curls and a tag around her neck saying who she was and where she was going. Plus, she said, "I can spell dog and cat." But she still felt shy, she said, because, "This is my first day."

"What are you shy about?" I asked.

"Boys."

"What is it about boys that makes you feel shy?"

"I'm a girl."

Then the buses pulled in and suddenly a hundred little kids were piling out. Matt Mollon, a father with a video camera, pointed it at his son, Joel, to capture this moment of history. I asked Matt if I could interview Joel, and he agreed. Here's what I wrote him:

I WANT TO BE A BIRD

Joel Mollon's first day of kindergarten looks pretty good so far. His dad showed up to videotape him. Joel liked that. And he thinks school will be good. He doesn't really know what will happen, though. And he doesn't know exactly what he wants to be when he grows up. But he has some ideas.

"Maybe a fire fighter," he says. "Or a bird trainer. Or maybe a bird."

A BIRD???

"They fly around in the yard and pick up worms. I wish I could be a bird. Then I could fly around in the sky."

But the big question before he goes to class is: WOULD HE LIKE TO EAT WORMS???

"Noooo!"

Joel Mollon on his first day of kindergarten.

Within ten minutes, all the kids were lined up and marched into school. At that moment, I realized I'd lost my black-and-gold Cross pen. Mike Grabske, the principal, looked on the gravel lot where I'd written Joel's story and found it in twenty seconds. Mike told me that counting his twenty-five years as principal of the school, his ten years in education before that, plus his six years in college and graduate school and thirteen years in elementary and secondary school, all totaled he'd spent fifty-four years in school.

"I look forward to every year more and more," he said, "because you never know when it might be your last. And the first day of school is probably the most exciting day of the whole year. You see the enthusiasm. Bright colors, new clothes, everybody looking forward to the new year."

As if he could see the new year spreading out beyond the horizon, he gazed at the hills to the south of the school and said, "This is probably the third- or fourth-highest elevation in the lower peninsula. On a clear day you can see Canada to the east and Detroit to the south. You probably never noticed that."

Ever the teacher.

"I'm lost!" came a voice from behind us.

I turned around to see little Joel with tears rolling down his cheeks.

"Everybody went inside, and I don't know where they went!"

Mr. Grabske took him to his class, and I followed. Joel's teacher, Mrs. Petzgold, gave me permission to write a 60-Second Novel for the whole class. As she went about her

business introducing the children to their fate for the next
thirteen years, I sat in one of the child-sized chairs and typed:

ALREADY THE FIRST MINUTE OF SCHOOL IS PAST

Millions and billions of years passed by
before the first day of kindergarten
arrived for Joel, Casey, Patrick, Brian,
Jamie, Nicole and the other kids in Mrs.
Petzgold's class at Indian Hills Elementary
School.
They all have their name tags on now.
"Can we play now?" asks Maria.
"Not yet," says Mrs. Petzgold.
A little boy isn't on Mrs. Petzgold's
list, so she takes him to the office to see
where he belongs. While she's away, the kids
tell a visitor what they'll be when they
grow up.
"A dentist," says Jessica.
"A ballerina," says Stephanie.
Now Mrs. Petzgold is back, leading them
in singing "If you're happy and you know
it." First they clap, then they jump up and
down, then they turn around, then they
raise their arms high, then low, then they
squat down, then get up.
"Okay," says Mrs. Petzgold, "what we're
going to do next, does everybody see that
flag? We're going to face the flag, and put
our right hand over our heart. Does everybody know where the heart is, where it's
beating? Then we're going to say a short
one: 'Red, white and blue, I love you.'"
After billions of years of waiting, the
first minute of school forxthexxxxhildren
is now already past. But the 22 children
in Mrs. Petzgold's class will remember it
forever and ever.

After I read the story aloud, little Jessica said, "Maria was the one who said she wanted to be a dentist, not me." Everybody's a critic.

Mrs. Petzgold said, "Oh, that's a very good story!" exactly as she might have said to one of her students.

Outside, the insufferable humidity and heat of the day before had been blown away. It was in the low eighties, with a piercing promising sky so clear, I could almost see graduation day.

The Crack Runner

From the innocence of Romeo I drove to Detroit, where I met an old college friend for lunch. I told him I wanted to visit the worst possible section of the city to write a 60-Second Novel for somebody. "Cass Street," Dave said with assurance. "Just keep going on it, and the farther you go, the weirder it gets."

I drove a few miles, looking for the weirdest-looking corner I could find, then doubled back to an abandoned, trashed-out Victorian building, where a skinny hooker paced across the street and a group of men sat on the stoop.

"Hey man, can you lend me two bucks?" asked a thin guy as I walked up wearing my bow tie and carrying my typewriter. I told him I was traveling across the country to interview people and write their instant life stories. "I'll talk to you for two bucks," he said, but I wouldn't do it.

I started walking away from him as three more guys came down the street, one of them as huge and broad as a circus strongman. Passing by me, he touched behind my ear with his wet thumb—the old "wet willy." I didn't let it rattle me, but I did worry that I was getting surrounded. Then another guy up the block a few steps said, "Hey, are you with the Census?" I hurried over to him and explained what I was doing. "I'll tell you my story," he said, "but come over to the church. You'll get a lottery ticket here."

"A what?"

"A lottery ticket. You know, a ticket from the police. They come by every hour and twenty minutes and give tickets to whoever's standing around."

I feared I was getting set up by going over to the church,

but it looked legitimate, and lots of ordinary people were walking in and out of the place. So I followed him.

"I'm Patrick," he said, and began describing just how bad the area really was. The more he talked, the more I wondered if I'd been insane for coming to such a dangerous area. He seemed so nice, though. He had a bump on his head, as though he'd fallen recently. One particular line in his story really grabbed me, which I used as the title.

THE WORLD I'M IN IS NOT THE REAL WORLD

Patrick has lived on this corner of Cass
and Alexandrian in Detroit for nineteen years.
"You can't go xxxx no lower than this,"
he says. It's too dangerous for his visitor
to stand on the corner, Patrick says, so he
takes the visitor half a block over to the
Cass Methodist Church.
Patrick had three brothers killed right
on that corner.
"But I'm still here," he says. "I've got
nowhere else to go. I know xx the world I'm
in is not the real world, but I'd be a
misfit in the real world."
Patrick makes his living as a runner. He
wakes up about nine and asks the dealers on
the stroll who needs help. Mostly at this
corner they sell "dooshee," which is heroin,
but they call it that to "fool the man."
Then they've got xxxxxx "mix and roll. Mix is
flour. Doosh is rock."
It's hard to understand it all. He's
right; it is like another world.
Yet Patrick seems like a nice guy. "I'm
single," he says. "I never been married, I
don't have kids. I haven't had no reason to
change. So I'm just out here like the rest
of them on a suicidal mission. That's all
it is. It's going to happen sooner or later.
It's a matter of fact. I don't have time to
worry about it. I gotta keep my eye on this
guy, that alley, that car, this truck. I
just hope when I do get popped I got some
luck enough to duck one of those bullets.
Somebody get popped every day, every other
night on this corner."
Good luck and Godspeed, Patrick. May
you find your way to the real world.

After I finished reading the story to him, he commented, "I'd never leave this place for anything. I love it here. It's so alive. I'm forty-eight, and if I didn't live here I'd probably be walking with a cane and looking like an old man. I love the excitement."

When we stood up to go, he winced. "I got popped in the leg a few weeks ago," he said. "Makes it hard to get up."

We shook hands and said good-bye, and I hurried back to my car, glad to find it still there with the radio intact.

Minute People

On the last day of my trip across America, I saw a sign outside Boston that made me burst out laughing:

Minute Man National Historic Park

I took the exit, and soon found myself in Concord, Massachusetts. Studying a historic map of the town, I learned that here, within a mile of each other in the second half of the nineteenth century, had lived Ralph Waldo Emerson, Henry David Thoreau, Nathaniel Hawthorne and Louisa May Alcott. Thoreau's cabin was barely a mile and a half outside town. And now all four of them rested within a couple hundred feet of each other in the town's Sleepy Hollow Cemetery.

I drove over to the cemetery, took out my Remington, and carried it to Thoreau's grave. I sat on the grass and wrote this paean to four of America's greatest writers:

EMERSON, ALCOTT, HAWTHORNE, THOREAU

So close together they lie! These
geniuses of American literature, bunched like
a few sweet Red Delicious on America's vast
crab apple tree of democracy. How comes it
that we, with our VCRs and our Apple IIs and
our car phones and our millions of college
graduates, cannot equal in a quarter century
what they churned out in a quarter year?
Neighbors they were, selling their houses to
each other. One wants to say, "It's as though
Louisa May Alcott lived next door to ~~Hawkhorn~~
Hawthorne, who lived down the road from
Thoreau and Emerson," when that's precisely
the case. What divine seed gave birth to such
~~qama~~ quadruplets? What egg, Louisa dear, grew
to such dinosaur proportions? O to go back,
to live there with them, to borrow a few
dollars from Emerson and walk a few miles to
Walden Pond, that a country might find some
solitude and self-reliance! To kick through
their leaves of grass, for ours have grown
brown and thin, with a thousand signs
sprouting up each Spring saying, "Keep Off!"
To ask them, "What did you know that we do
not? What did you have that we have lost?"
But our wishes are not in vain, our prayers
go not unanswered. For they were not painters
whose colors fade and peel. They were not
soldiers, whose bullets fall and whose
shots—heard 'round the world though they
may have been—are deafened by time's thick
~~muffler~~ muzzle. They were writers, whose
words never alter, never corrode, never
dampen, never chip, never stain, never die.
And closer than they lived in mortal life,
they stand eternally on bookshelves, and in
the hands of a child who evermore can read
them, talk with them, walk to the woods with
them, to find that softly, stealthily, they
have become us.

I placed the story against Thoreau's grave, snapped a picture and left. As I began the long drive home to Brooklyn, watching again the familiar red taillights of the cars ahead of me, and the warm blue-lit dial of my radio, I realized that the trip I'd intended as a fond farewell to this wacko career had instead turned into a confirmation.

Chapter 11

Life and Death

Whether on the sidewalks of Chicago or in the middle of a gaudy New York City party, perfect strangers have told me their most intensely private experiences about the love of their life, the death of their child, the loss of their spouse. I learned death is just another part of the great story of life. Writing "the end" to our own life story is our final and greatest challenge.

At a sixtieth birthday party, I was wandering the room when an elderly woman waved me over. I carried my typewriter and sat down in an empty seat beside her. By this late hour in the party, most of the people were up on the dance floor.

"Where's your husband?" I asked.

"He couldn't make it," she said. "He's the commodore of our yacht club, and they had a function he couldn't miss."

Things started out lightly enough, but the longer we talked, the deeper we got. "You're like a priest," she said, squeezing my hand.

By the end, when I finished typing her story, she took it from me and said, "I'll read this when I get home." Here's the story I wrote for her:

BOATING IN THE FOG

Emily and George have one appearance when they're out on the town. He's friendly, outgoing, happy. She's more quiet and shy.

But when they get home, it's the opposite. George is quiet. She is more outgoing when it's just the two of them.

You see, she's happy with who she is, very secure. George, though, seems kind of sad at home. And he has reasons.

Their two children have both passed away. First their son, of natural causes, then their daughter, in a boating accident. Who would have thought it possible?

Now Emily, after a thing like this, looked into herself to find what is there. She still had her God, herself, her husband, her friends, and she still had her son and daughter. They never left her--not really. And she can talk about it, face it, accept it.

George seems not to have done that yet. He goes out drinking. It's so understandable.

And yet isn't he the commodore of their California yacht club? Surely he should know how to navigate in the fog: by the buoys, the fog horns, the lights. For those buoys, those lights are his wife, his children and his God.

In the fog of this world, George can no longer see them.

But he is not lost. Emily can see him still, drifting by. If only he would reach out his hand.

At Higbee's department store in Cleveland, I met a woman named Joyce on a September afternoon in 1990.

A NEW BEGINNING

Joyce just finished chemotherapy on Monxxlx Monday and Tuesday. She had uterine cancer. The surgeon got it all out, so he gave her only a little bit of chemo--not enough to ma ke her hair fall out. They caught it early. When she was j walking around in the hospital, which the doctors told her to do before they discharged her, she saw three women getting chemo, one with a towel around her head , two with nothing but peach fuzz. She knew that could have been her. But she knew, too, that by saving her, God must have something in store for her. There's something she's supposed to do, although she doesn't kxxx yet know what.

Her friend, Ginny, had cancer last year. And Joyce tried to be a good friend to her, and wondered, "What if it were me?" And she watched as Ginny learned a great lesson from this: to take time for herself and have a little fun. If her kids wanted dinner at 6pm sharp and she wasn't ready, she told them to cook it kxx themselves. "Here's the pan, there's the stove, hop to it, boys," she told them. One day a week was for her. If God gets His day, surely Ginny deserves hers.

So now they've both found a new beginning. It's as though life were put through the washer in Liquid All: the brights are brighter, the joys more joyful, the warmth

warmer. So even if Joyce just goes home and
eats a bag of potato chips, it will be a
beautiful wonderful moving experience. Doing
the laundry will bring tears to her eyes.
Taking out the garbage will be a religious
experience.

Because everything old is new again. And
that such wonder can come from a rotten no-
good thing like cancer: this is a miracle.

Dan Hurley

At a party on November 23, 1996, I met a woman in her seventies named Sonia, who spent nearly fifteen minutes telling me how she met her husband. "It's a long story," she warned me, but I listened.

THAT'S A LONG STORY

Sonia was in Auschwitz, where she met this woman in her 40s, named Basha. Basha treated Sonia like she was her daughter, because Sonia was all alone. Sonia's two sisters had been killed.

When the war ended, and the gates of Auschwitz were opened, Basha went to look for her son. She told Sonia, "If I find my son, you will be my daughter-in-law."

Sonia went one way, Basha went another. Finally Basha found her son, Morris.

"I found a girl for you," Basha told Morris. "Her name is Sonia."

The mother and son went from town to town, along with the other refugees. One day Morris fell asleep on the train. When he woke up, he got off the train and went to find the Jews who lived in this place. He managed to find the people from Bialystock. And there he found Sonia.

From that day on, he didn't let her go. It's been 51 years now.

"We care for each other, we love each other, we care now more than we did when we were young."

Sonia is right. It was a long story. And a very happy one.

On September 21, 1992, I wrote novels at a party in
Connecticut for Delancey Street, a drug rehabilitation
program. Instead of the usual suspects who show up at ritzy
parties—the doctors, the lawyers, the business executives—I
had the opportunity to speak to many of Delancey Street's
recovering addicts, including a man named Joseph.

Back Toward His Dreams

Joseph had dreams. Some people don't
have even that much in life, but Joseph at
least had dreams.
He dreamed of being in California, in
Los Angeles, driving down the freeway with
a car phone, talking to a producer.
"Listen, baby," he'd be saying, "get back
to me, I'm busy right now."
It'd be lights, camera, action all the
way. And heavy on the action.
But somewhere his dreams took a left
turn and were trapped in a traffic jam. He
went to college, but then his beloved Mom
took sick. He went home and forgot about
school. After a long and bitter illness,
she died. One morning soon after the
funeral, Joseph woke up in jail. He had
robbed a social club. He had gotten into
booze. He had forgotten his dreams. His
mother was gone, and he was ready to follow.
But then, when his time in jail was done
and he started doing the same old things,
it happened.
Something pulled at his sleeve.
"Leave me alone," he said, and tried to
walk away. But it pulled at the leg of his
trousers.

His dreams.
His hopes.
His future.
His father and his mother and the way
he'd always thought life would be.
Finally he stopped and turned and faced
down his dreams.
"Okay, so who are you, Mr. Big Stuff,"
he asked, "and what do you want?"
But there was nothing there.
Just the wind, whistling empty.
So Joseph went to Delancey Street, to
see if he could find where his dreams had
gone.
And it's a long, hard road.
But Joseph has started. And all that
matters now is that he sticks on the road
to reach them.

At a party in June of 1998, I began talking with a young man about his business and his kids. He mentioned that it was a particularly stressful time for him, because his dad was sick. "I'm going to the hospital to see him right after the party," he said. He began telling me all about his dad, and what he was going through—the pain and the heartache. And so I wrote:

```
            ALL FOR THE BEST


     Things tend to work out for the best,
one way or another. Like when the company
Robert worked for decided to close down
the location where he worked, he and some
partners decided to start their own com-
pany. Since then Robert's income has gone up
50 percent.
     Now Robert's dad, Robert senior, is very
sick. He's actually on a respirator, with
kidney failure. It's getting pretty grim.
Joseph goes from work to the hospital. His
dad can just barely acknowledge his presence.
     Could the process of aging, getting old
and sick and dying, possibly be all for the
best? Because if people didn't get old and
pass on, how could a new generation come
along on their heels? It's a huge process
that unfolds, each generation ceding its
place to the next. Robert knows it was his
father who made him the good person he is.
His dad didn't have it easy, their mom was
sick when they were young, but his dad took
ca re of her and his business and everyone.
Robert learned the importance of family from
him. That's why, when he walks in the door
to his home and his own kids run up yelling
"Daddy daddy," Robert feels it makes it xx
all xxx worthwhile. And so if one father is
coming in the door, and another walking out,
who's to say that in God's plan, maybe it's
all for the best?
     Although at a time like this, it might
not feel that way.
```

In response to someone's loss of a loved one, it's so hard to know what to say. I know I could never say the kinds of things my typewriter comes up with, as it did for a woman named Anne whom I met at a party in 1996.

TAILSPIN

Anne was a fairly happy-go-lucky young woman when, at the age of 27, her younger brother died in a plane crash. This put Anne into quite a tailspin of her own. She became given over to saying things like, "You can't depend on anything in this world." Death had crept like a beetle in the night up the vine of her life, to eat on the tender green shoots of her faith. The emptiness of it all--what the heck was the point of it all, when loss comes so suddenly, without warning?

And so Anne shuffled along, the moon ever in her sky. Even during a picnic, even at a happy party, thoughts of the end invaded her mind--like ants at the picnic, indeed.

Just when she thought she was coming to grips with it all, her mother died. And then her father died.

Was there no end to it?

No, there is no end to it. Or rather, there is always an end to everything. We are all of us headed that way.

But why, Anne asked. Who the hell worked out such a sick scheme anyway?

And then wisdom came to Anne: not understanding, but acceptance. She would not clap and applaud all the facts of life, but she could no longer deny them.

And from then on the briefness of life
became to her a call: to enjoy it while
she's here, to make the best of things,
to honor those who came before, and
leave the world a better place for those
to follow. For then, when she does go,
and joins all the others, she will look
back out the rearview mirror of her life
and say, "What a beautiful, beautiful
ride it was."

Dan Hurley

Chapter 12

Tall Story

As the ten-year anniversary of my first 60-Second Novel approached, I wanted to fulfill another crazy dream that had haunted me for most of the decade: to write a novel from the roof of a New York City skyscraper on a single sheet of paper that slowly descends to the sidewalk below.

At the time I was executive vice president of the American Society of Journalists and Authors, headquartered in the old Paramount Building in the heart of Times Square. In January of 1993, I broached

the idea with the executive director, as a "write-a-thon" fund-raiser for ASJA's charitable trust. I suggested that I could do it from the eighteenth-floor setback roof

of the building, and people could pledge so much per foot of writing. To my amazement, she liked the idea and said, why not? So she asked the building management what they thought, and they liked it, too.

Uh-oh. It was beginning to look like I might actually have to carry out this madcap escapade.

I went to the executive council of ASJA, and they also said they loved it. Didn't anybody know this was nuts?

First I had to find a video designer, because I wanted to communicate with people on the sidewalk below via a two-way interactive video system. Bob Holman of the Nuyorican Poetry Cafe put me in touch with a video guy, who put me in touch with another video guy, who put me in touch with Richard Reta, of the New York University video department. Richard brought in his girlfriend, Dawnja Burris. Together they turned out to be the perfect crew: consummate professionals and totally enthused.

Then I had to find myself an engineer, because the building management had three conditions: they wanted me to get it approved by all appropriate agencies. They wanted me to get a licensed engineer to design it. And they wanted me to get insurance.

I found an engineer named Gus Patel, who promised he could do the whole thing for just $500. While he was working up a design, I received approval from the local police sergeant, got insured under a rider to ASJA's business insurance, put together a P.R. list, and placed an announcement about the event in the ASJA calendar. After that, it would have been embarrassing to pull out.

The building's engineer reviewed Gus's design, and that's when the problems began. He didn't like Gus's plan at all. All the details were missing, he said: not only of exact weights and wind pressures, but of the exact hardware. What type of paper? What type of cables to secure the paper and prevent it from blowing down onto the street? How would the paper be attached to the cables?

So Gus went back to the drawing board. A few days later, he called to tell me that a city agency required a master rigger to put up the steel cables that would hold the paper in place. He received a quote from a master rigger: $2,000. That's when I flipped, because I was already spending $500 on Gus, $500 on the video equipment, and at least another $1,000 on materials and promotion. This thing was edging toward $5,000 in expenses.

I called other riggers, and finally was referred to Auer's, who quoted me a price of $1,800. It would have to do.

I began researching what kind of paper could be used. My

original idea was to use a long roll of computer printout paper, sandwiched in a double layer of plastic. I called a banner company, but they said it would be blown apart by the wind.

Two weeks to go.

So then my brother Mike told me about something called Tyvek, this supposedly unrippable paper made by DuPont, the same material used in unrippable envelopes. I called DuPont, asked about buying Tyvek, and was referred to an expert in their company. He said yes, it should work, and faxed me information about it. But he turned out to be not as much of an expert on Tyvek as another guy at DuPont, Rick Galloway.

But Rick Galloway was not in his office the entire day I called, and called, and called. I feared he might be unreachable, but I had to reach him. Sitting in the ASJA office on that Thursday evening—just eight nights until the event—I decided to find his home and call him there. Someone in his office had said Rick lived "down south," and since the plant was in Delaware, I began with Virginia, trying to get his home number.

There was no listing for him in northern Virginia.

Then I called southern Virginia, and eureka, there he was. His wife answered the phone, and said he was in Luxembourg or some such place, but that he was coming home that night. I asked her to take a message and told her it was urgent.

Bless his soul, Rick Galloway called me the next morning at a quarter to seven. He told me exactly how to fix the system, and everything I needed. He told me that I had to put something called "edging" on the edges of the paper to prevent it from ripping in the wind, and he said I had to put "corner guards" around the holes that the rings would go through, attaching the paper to the cables.

I called the building engineer to let him know how things were going, and he told me he didn't think I could get everything completed in time. He suggested I push the date back. But I didn't listen. I kept pushing all my people for answers, for solutions. I wasn't going to let anybody tell me my dream couldn't happen.

I went back to looking for the rings connecting the paper to the cables. I thought of maybe some kind of mountain-climbing equipment, those things they use to connect themselves to their ropes. I drove an hour to a big mountain-climbing store, but the things turned out to cost five bucks apiece—and I needed a hundred. Then I thought maybe a boating supply store would have some sort of tackle, and drove out to a place on the edge of the Hudson River. But that was too heavy and too expensive.

Then I flashed on something so simple: key rings! And so on Thursday, on my way to meet the building engineer, I stopped in a key shop and saw a two-inch-wide key ring that was perfect. I bought ten right there, and ordered one hundred more.

I went to the engineer with the new design by Gus, the

Tyvek paper, the corner guard sample and the key ring attachment. "You see how far along your idea has come?" he said. "Your original idea would not have worked."

He wanted to look at our plans over the weekend, and then meet with me, Gus, the building manager, the building superintendent, the rigger and the video designers on Tuesday. I called up a paper supply place to order the roll of Tyvek, the corner guards and the edging. But nobody had the corner guards. DuPont told me to call a company named Tecra, and Tecra told me the names of stores to call. Finally I found a place that said they had them and would ship them, but an hour later they called back and said it was all a mistake and they didn't have them.

So I called another place, and another place, and a third place. This one lady told me on the phone on Monday—just five days before the event scheduled for Friday, May 21—that she had sent the order to Tecra and it was being shipped to her store.

"But can it get to me by Friday?" I asked her. "I need it by Friday."

"I think so," she said, "but I can't guarantee it."

And I started yelling at this poor lady: *"I need to know if you can get me the corner guards by Friday!"*

She gave me her supervisor, the owner, who explained it was almost definite. But just the same, I called one more place, in Boston. They also had them and could get them for me if this place backed out.

Tuesday afternoon rolled around. The building engineer and the super and the building manager questioned me, Gus and Richard. It was like oral exams for law school. But we answered every question, and at the end of that meeting, all systems were go.

T-minus sixty-three hours and counting.

After the big meeting, I wanted to fax out the full, final press releases, but the fax in the ASJA office was broken. So on Wednesday I had to rush over to pay with my credit card for the video monitors, and then stop by the fax place on 13th Street, and it cost me eighty-six dollars for the faxes alone. Meanwhile *New York Newsday* wanted to send a photographer to shoot me in front of the building.

With a camera.

By now I was running around everywhere like a psycho. I had to buy fishing tackle to use as a "tag line," to pull the paper down if it got stuck. I picked up the one hundred key rings, and then went to pick up the Tyvek paper from the place that was cutting it down to the proper size, so that it was just the right width to feed through my typewriter. Back at our apartment, Alice, two friends and my father-in-law were waiting to prepare the paper with the edging strips, to make it stronger.

But when I showed up at the paper-cutting place at 7:00 P.M. as scheduled, it was closed. I circled the building, looking for signs of life, but the lights were out, the parking lot empty. Like an unstoppable machine, I went to a pay phone and convinced the operator to place an emergency call to the home of the paper cutter's unlisted phone number. He wasn't home.

I wouldn't be able to get the paper until Thursday morning, so with nothing else to do, my friends went home. But I could handle it. A nuclear bomb could have fallen on Manhattan at that point and I would have handled it. I spent the evening trying to find someone who could spend all day Thursday preparing the paper. I ended up finding the daughter of a friend, who wanted ten dollars an hour. Hired!

I picked the paper up on Thursday morning, at 8:30 A.M., and then the young woman I'd hired spent ten hours, all day Thursday, processing it. When I came home at ten o'clock Thursday night—the night before the event—she had finished. I had my key rings, my corner guards (which were UPS'ed to the ASJA office) and my paper. I had met with Richard and Dawnja to work out the final details on the video. The press releases were out, the insurance forms were in, everything was ready.

I went to bed at midnight, so wound-up and excited that I couldn't fall asleep. I tossed and turned until 4:30 A.M., when I was supposed to get up in preparation for the 6:00 A.M. beginning of the eighteen-hour writing marathon, which I had dubbed "Tall Story: A Novel in 18 Stories."

After five straight days of rain, the sun rose into the clear blue sky visible above a Calvin Klein underwear billboard just as we arrived on the roof. Joining me up on the roof all day, attaching the paper to the key rings and the key

rings to the steel cables, was my old friend, Brian Dunleavy. Soon one news media crew after another was making the sojourn up to interview me: CNN, WABC, WCBS, WNBC, the Associated Press, the *Daily News*, and

"Tall Story" was covered live on the evening news.

the *New York Post.* The New York affiliate for CBS even broadcast live from the roof during the six o'clock news.

More importantly, thousands of New Yorkers had a direct experience of interacting with a writer crazed enough to make his loony vision of interactive literature come true.

As I started, two minor technical glitches prevented me from speaking with passersby on the street below: The video connection wasn't working, and the audio wasn't working. But I pressed on, writing whatever came, keeping it moving one story (in both senses of the word) per hour so that the paper would descend all eighteen stories (196 feet) by midnight. And make it I did: exhausted but exhilarated. The following excerpts, transcribed from the original roll of Tyvek paper which now hangs from the top of my office bookshelf, capture some of what went on:

7 a.m./Second Story: Care and Feeding

....And so I face 7 a.m. with the hope
that the day will bring more than just ~~another~~
another hot shower and breakfast and
shave and cup of coffee.
For I need a shave. I need a hot shower.
Lord knows, I need a cup of coffee. I need
breakfast. Yes, and I need about 14 hours
of sleep.
But I need so much more than these mere
things.
For sometimes, we have more important
things to do than merely sleep.
And today, I am writing a novel from
the roof.
Yet it is done for the care and feeding
of the human spirit.
Of the author's spirit.
And of everyone else's spirit.
We all need a bit of absurdity in our
lives.
We all need a bit of madness.
It's the madness that keeps us sane.
GOOD
MORNING!
HOW
ARE YOU?
ANSWER
IF YOU
CAN HEAR.

"No," they say, but they can see what I'm
writing on the TV screen. They can hear
only what my fingers are saying.

Hello Alice, my wife.

So, Alice, what do you think of this?

Alice says, "Carpe Diem," which means,
"Seize the day."

"I think it's really wonderful," says
the lovely Alice.

That's why I married her. For the care
and feeding of my soul.

Kids, cops and MTV receptionists all took their turn becoming part of my Tall Story.

9 a.m./Fourth Story:
   WORKADAY

Santos is a messenger.
Everyone I've talked to today
seems to be a messenger.
    If you're a messenger, Santos,
what is your message?
    WHAT IS YOUR MESSAGE?
    I am asking Santos to read the
question that I've written. A
video camera behind my shoulder is
focused on what I'm writing.
    At least somebody is focused on
what I'm writing.
    And a giant TV screen on the
sidewalk below is broadcasting from
the video camera, showing what I
write as I write it. But Santos is
not answering the question I have
written here.
    "I can't read so good," he says.
    "Can you read in Spanish?" I ask.
    "Not that good," he says.
    "So basically you can't read?"
    "I'm illiterate."
    This may be a first: literature
for illiterates. But Santos would
like to read. He's going to a
program in Far Rockaway to help
him learn. So now we shall ask him
aloud: "Santos, since you're a
messenger, what is your message?"
    And Santos replies: "My message
is for God to help me to learn how
to read."
    God will teach, if Santos will learn.

2 p.m./Ninth Story:
THE HIGHER POWER HOUR

How did I manage to pick the one sunny
day of the week, after an entire week of
rain and clouds and cold?
    Andrea thinks it's pure luck. She thinks
I was just lucky to have picked this day.
    But luck had nothing to do with it.
    You see, since I'm writing this hour
about matters spiritual, I should say that I
have felt a higher calling for many years to
write these 60-Second Novels.
    This past Sunday, when I was all
frightened and nervous about the event, I
prayed to God in church. Sometimes when I
pray, I have these intensely imagined exper-
iences--or are they imagined?--of God talking
to me, or showing me things. Somewhat like
hallucinations or dreams.
    So this Sunday, I asked in my prayers,
"Is this insane? Am I crazy? Am I wasting my
time and money for nothing?"
    And you know what I heard as God's answer?
    God laughed. Or at least I heard God
laughing a big jolly belly laugh, and he gave
me a hug and told me that he thought what I'm
doing is wonderful, that he wishes more
people would get involved in such whimsical
crazy things. He delighted in what I was
setting out to do. And it felt just like being
hugged by my father, who is no longer living.
    So the upshot is, I know it was not just
luck that this day proved so glorious and
sunny and warm.
    It is only heaven shining down happily
upon me.

4 p.m./ Eleventh Hour:
END OF THE WORK WEEK

Jeffrey is an opera singer. He is both a
student and a performer, having sung at the
Met, City Opera, and in Europe. This week
he just finished his exams, but his work is
not done. It's the end of the work week for
some, but not for him. He keeps working. He
keeps learning. Until his last breath, he'll
keep going.

He's a man full of surprises. One does xx
not often see a black opera singer, and he
has learned to expect people to be surprised.
AND he seems kind of sick of it. Why should
they be surprised? Why can't a black man
sing opera?

When I said to him that it seemed natural
to me that black men should sing opera,
since they often seem to have deeper, more
resonant voices than many white guys, he
replied, "It's the watermelon and the
fried chicken."

This was the kind of reaction I remember
getting in Monument Valley, Utah, when I
was traveling across America with Alice and
met a group of Native Americans. They were
offering horse rides for $25. And while we
rode with them, we asked them questions
about their lives. And they reacted quite
sarcastically.

When Alice, who loves to talk about food,
asked them what they like to eat, they
replied, "We drink cold coffee and eat
beans out of a can."

When I asked who owns the reservation,
they said, "We all do. We can do whatever
we want to it. If we want to build a casino

on top of the mountain, we can do that. And
then all the tourists can come and fall off."

I had felt bad that he was assuming that
our own curious questions were rude, or
ignorant. He seemed to be sick of the
presumptions of white men. He was sick of
the prejudices, the caricatures.

He was sick of being reduced to a
wigwam and a blanket.

And it seems to me now that Jeffrey
has some of that same anger and annoyance
at the presumptions and prejudices being
dumped on him. He wants to be accepted on
his own terms, as who he is. He wants to
define himself _for_ himself, and not have
others define him.

As the 60-Second Novelist, I have
experienced the same thing. People are
always wondering what the hell I'm doing
with the typewriter. "Why are you doing
that?" they ask. "Are you a writer? Don't
you want to do REAL writing someday?"

And they can't understand that for me
this IS real writing, that this for me is
the best writing I could possibly do. I've
written articles for The New York Times and
Good Housekeeping and People and New York
and TV Guide, but for me the best thing
I've ever done is this writing on the streets
for ordinary people one at a time.

And so maybe it's our lot, Jeffrey,
for all of us humans to be misunderstood.

Not just blacks.

Not just Native Americans.

Not just 60-Second Novelists.

But anyone who is trying to break the
rules, trying to define his or her own
life, trying to find his or her own soul and

follow his or her own path.

No one ever said it would be easy.

And no one ever said that everybody would stand and applaud our efforts.

Or that they would even understand.

And why do they need to understand?

We're doing it for ourselves, after all, not for anyone else. Which is why we should all of us remember the words of counsel once given to me by a very wise woman:

Be very understanding of their lack of understanding.

The "Tall Story" descends from the eighteenth-story roof toward the sidewalk below.

5 p.m./Twelfth Story:
RUSH HOUR

Milka lives
in the Bronx.
Milka wants
to rush away
from all the
bad influ-
ences in the
Bronx.
She wants
to rush away
from the
drug addicts.
She wants
to find
good, clean,
healthy
people. She
wants to find people who have
their head together. In the Bronx, she
says, she doesn't know anybody who has their
act together.

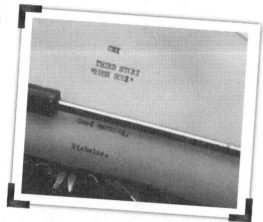

Not one person.
That's the world Milka lives in.
So in a few weeks she's moving on up to
a new way of living, a better part of town
where people have their act together. And
maybe then she'll be able to make some
friends.
Promise me this, Milka:
Make one good healthy friend who has
her act together.
Someone, in other words, exactly like
you.

10 p.m./Seventeenth Story:
    PARTY TIME

Now it's ten o'clock at night, and the
parties are starting.
An argument is brewing on the street now
among a group of blacks. They're arguing
over blacks versus whites, light-skinned
blacks versus dark-skinned blacks, and who
is "really" black.
One of them was talking peace and love
all the way, but now he seems to be the
loudest mouth on the block. With a peace
lover like him, who needs a nuclear
terrorist?
Yes, it's turning into the wild time
of the night, when the Wild Things come
out to play. People get a few brews into
them. They say something, they drink a
beer, and KABOOOOM, mental meltdown
occurs and the result is violence.
But we all want to party. We all
want to enjoy ourselves. And let me tell
you, I've enjoyed this immensely. This
has been the greatest party of my life.
This has been a pure piece of pleasure.
This has been the greatest treat to
myself that I've ever given myself.
As the gentlemen continue to yell
and shout at each other in a frighteningly
loud manner, up walks Henry from
Minnesota, the place where everybody gets
along well.
He is pleased to see this real-life
debate. To him, this is a real-life
"Town Hall," exactly the kind of thing
Ross Perot had in mind.

You know, bring the people together, to work out the differences between the Republican Party, the Democratic Party, and the Party-Hardy Party.

Just make sure you check your weapons at the door. Your weapons...and your inhibitions about shouting out loud.

Because this is not the marketplace of ideas.

This is the battlefield of thought.

I celebrate "Touchdown" of the novel at midnight. "I did it!"

Chapter 13

America's Biggest Sidewalk

Just when it seemed I had explored every setting possible (and impossible) for my instant writing, from street corners to department stores, from Iowa cornfields to Manhattan rooftops, along came a little company called America Online, announcing in late 1994 that they were actively seeking "infopreneurs" to develop creative interactive entertainment.

Hey, I was interactive before interactive was cool.

When I told some writer friends that I was going to apply, one of them said, "It'll never work. Nobody wants entertainment on the Internet."

In September 1995, "The 60-Second Novelist" site launched on AOL and did far better than

any sane person ever would have predicted. It was praised by *Wired, USA Today,* the *New York Times* and MSNBC, and was one of just three AOL sites featured in *24 Hours in Cyberspace.* Suddenly the low-tech guy with the manual typewriter was a cyber star.

In October 1996, I launched a new site, "The Amazing Instant Novelist," which continues to this day. Rather than making the site just an outlet for me, I use it to encourage others to express themselves with super-short stories, poems, opinions, humor, memoirs and more. Just as I found an instant outlet for my writing on the streets, hundreds of thousands of people have discovered that they can be instantly "published" on AOL at keyword "novel," or on the Internet at *www.instant novelist.com,* where their stories and poems can be seen by millions at the click of a mouse. It's the Nike "just do it" philosophy transplanted into the realm of creative expression.

But my live shows, in which I write instant novels online for whoever pops into my chat room, is the heart of the site. I was amazed from the beginning that I could usually get a sense of people's personalities just from reading what they typed into the computer in response to my questions. Online, it's literally a matter of reading between the lines to figure out who this person truly is.

The way it works is simple. I sit at my computer at home, doing this "show"—which amounts to nothing more than the text which I and others write—while an audience of anywhere from a dozen to as many as 900 people read it live on their computer screens. I write a line, hit "enter" on my keyboard, and a second later, *that* line shows up on the screens of whoever is tuned in. I write the next line, hit "enter," that line appears beneath the previous line—and so on. I pick one person at a time to interview and then write his or her instant novel as everybody watches it happen right before their eyes. It's a writer's fantasy come true: instant publication.

Here follow some of my favorite online novels, along with the chats that led up to them. E-mail addresses (or "screen names" as they're known on AOL) have been changed to protect privacy.

After the Fairy Tale Ends

Here is the online chat I had with a woman I'll call "NimbleNot" in December of 1996, and the story I wrote for her in response:

Hurley Dan: OK, who's next?

NimbleNot: I've been in all these terrible, abusive relationships for years. Now, I finally found the guy of my dreams, and I don't know how to act.

Hurley Dan: WELL OF COURSE YOU SHOULD DUMP HIM, RIGHT? :)

NimbleNot: Feels like it! Isn't that crazy?

Hurley Dan: Nimble, why were you in all those horrible relationships?

NimbleNot: I just kept choosing the same guy (different face). Alcoholics, mostly.

Hurley Dan: Mmm-hmmmm. And how'd you find this lucky guy, the good one?

NimbleNot: I met this man here online nearly a year ago. We live together now and he is wonderful.

Hurley Dan: Cool, an online romance :)

NimbleNot: I met him the first night I had AOL.

Hurley Dan: WOW, cool!

NimbleNot: But it's hard to trust him. I feel like a puppy that's been beaten too many times. If he raises his hand to pet me, I cringe.

Hurley Dan: So are you learning to relax and enjoy? Or do you see real danger of your running off and leaving him?

NimbleNot: I'm trying hard to stick with him. Our relationship seems boring because I know he'll be home at night, and he won't spend grocery money on drugs, etc. Isn't that sick?

Hurley Dan: Not sick, Nimble, just the truth. I've heard that many times from women in your position. Now let me write your story.

NimbleNot: Please let it have a happy ending.

Hurley Dan: I'll do my best. Your story is entitled . . .

Cinderella after the Fairy Tale Ends

You all know the story of Cinderella, who was trapped by her evil stepmother. . . . Finally she found the prince and lived the life of a happy princess.

But after the fairy tale ended, Cinderella grew restless. She remembered those old days, down on her knees. . . . She remembered how her stepmother would abuse her. Sometimes she had gotten a secret joy from the abusive comments.

And now here she sat with Mr. High and Mighty Prince. Every night he brought her another freaking bouquet of roses.

Finally one night she snapped.

"Enough with the darn roses!"

"My darling beloved, what doth trouble thee?" asked the good prince.

"Screw your medieval lovey-dovey talk!" she replied. "Let's go out to the disco!"

"But darling, I was building you a castle . . ."

So Cinderella left and ran off with Grumpy the Dwarf. He beat her and made her work twenty-four hours a day.

And then one night, she realized at last how wrong she had been. "When all your dreams come true and the fairy tale at last becomes real," she realized, "sometimes it's boring as heck."

And so she returned to her prince, who welcomed her back with open arms.

Brought Home by My Father

During my show on October 14, 1998, I made the unusual decision to write one story for two people. Here's exactly what transpired:

Hurley Dan: . . . OK, so for whom should I write the next story? :)

SABRINA108: DAN I WANT YOUR HELP. My son-in-law is dying of cancer at age thirty-three. He has three little babies who love him. It's the loss, the waiting, pure heartache

PEACH: Dan, one month ago, my live-in boyfriend woke up one morning and said "I'm moving to Denver," no notice or anything. He left me that same day.

Hurley Dan: OK, folks, here's what sounds interesting to me. Let's bring BOTH Peach AND Sabrina onstage to have ONE story for BOTH of them.

PEACH: That would be interesting

Hurley Dan: OK, so, Peach, why did your boyfriend leave??

PEACH: To live with Mommy and Daddy . . . to get a better job

Hurley Dan: How did you react to his departure?

PEACH: I yelled, screamed, cried, considered suicide . . . and now I'm glad he's gone

Hurley Dan: Wow, how close were you two, Peach? How long had the relationship been going?

PEACH: We lived together for six months, dated for two months before that. I have pretty intense, quick relationships

CRADLE: Peach, that's not enough time to know what size underwear he's wearing

Hurley Dan: And how quickly did he leave after he announced his intention?

PEACH: Half an hour

AMAZN Bill: Ouch.

PEACH: "My dad's on his way over with a truck to get my stuff." "What stuff?" I asked. "All of it," and he was gone. What can I say, I know how to pick 'em.

Hurley Dan: And Sabrina, why is the son-in-law dying? What KIND of cancer?

SABRINA108: He has cancer all through his body and his blood

Hurley Dan: How is your daughter holding up, Sabrina? Is she totally falling apart? Or is she a tough cookie who will find a way to get through?

SABRINA108: She is a tough cookie who will fall apart after.

Hurley Dan: And how much time do they give him, Sabrina?

SABRINA108: One month ago, they gave him three weeks to two months

Hurley Dan: How long has your daughter been with him?

SABRINA108: Twelve years. they have a great relationship. My son-in-law is a good man, sensitive and very protective of his family. I feel such a heavy heart within me. When I look at my grandchildren it hurts so.

Hurley Dan: OK, guys . . . I'm ready to write one story for the both of you. And the story is entitled. . . .

Brought Home by My Father

The announcement came so suddenly.
I thought we would have days and months and years.
We were to grow old together.
We were to rock grandchildren on our knees.
Time rolled out before us like an interstate highway.
And then your father called.
"My father is coming to take me home," you said.
I did not want you to go.
I cried and begged your father that you should stay.
I needed you.
We all needed you.
But your father said he has a special plan for you.
He wants you near him.
He needs you back home.
I thought this was your home.
But your father, your jealous father—it was always his
home that was yours first and last.
It was from his home that you came.
And to his home you must return.
And so farewell, sweet lover.
The father has great things in store for you.
And be sure that when you return home with him
That you prepare a room for me
For one day I shall follow you home
As shall we all.

A Little Girl's Questions

Here is a chat I had on October 21, 1998, with a woman who was concerned about her little girl's questions, and the story that resulted:

LC8: My daughter muttered in her sleep, "I don't have a daddy." I have also heard her say that her Daddy is dead, which is not true.

Hurley Dan: Hmmm, how old is your daughter, LC?

LC8: Six. But I think that she has a lot of questions, and I don't know how to answer them.

Hurley Dan: Why would your daughter think she has no dad?

LC8: Well, he hasn't seen her dad since she was eleven months old and most of her friends are in families with a mom and a dad. She only knows my side of the family.

Hurley Dan: OK, so your daughter is saying she has no daddy, and for all practical purposes, that's true.

LC8: Yes—but she does have a grandfather and uncles and cousins who love her a lot.

Hurley Dan: What are her questions about? "Where's my dad?"

LC8: Yes, and why doesn't he contact me.

Hurley Dan: Those are perfectly reasonable questions for her. What do you tell her?

LC8: That her father loves her, but he hasn't seen her.

Hurley Dan: Her father loves her? Doesn't sound like it to me.

LC8: Well, I tell her that because I thought that it would be better. But basically he is a liar and so self-absorbed that he hasn't faced her since she was a baby. Sometimes I think he would be better off dead.

Hurley Dan: OK. So he is a jerk. How is your life otherwise these days?

LC8: I teach and she goes to daycare after school, so she is not alone. Also she and I do everything together, and there is my family.

Hurley Dan: May I ask for a first name for you and your daughter please, to use in the story? :)

LC8: My name is Linda and my daughter is Catherine

Hurley Dan: OK, now I'll try to write a story for Linda and Catherine. And the title of your story is:

A Little Girl's Questions

Catherine was just six years old, and she had many questions.

She wanted to know why Daddy wasn't around.

She wanted to know why he didn't visit.

She wanted to know why she didn't have what every girl deserves.

Linda searched for answers.

She was sure she could find an answer somewhere.

She looked under the couch.

She checked behind the radiator.

She dug around in the bottom of her old winter jacket's pocket.

She got down on her knees and looked under the bed.

But nowhere did she find the answers.

"My little girl," she said at last to her daughter, "There are some questions in this world for which there are no answers.

"But I do know this.

"You will never have to ask where I am.

"You will never have to wonder if I love you.

"You will never have to ask where your next meal is coming from.

"And you will never EVER have to ask why I love you so much.

"Because my love for you is something you need never question."

All My Children. . . .

On December 2, 1998, I chatted with a great-grandmother who still felt incomplete over the death of her dad back when she was a teenager. Here is how the chat, and the story, developed:

Hurley Dan: So who's next???

Mathely: How about me, Dan. I go to school fifteen hours a week, work forty, deal with a lot of stress and want to get married. I also have a fifteen-year-old granddaughter with me who has a baby son and I have custody.

Hurley Dan: So are you also building a pyramid in your spare time?

AMAZN Bill: I wonder where all the stress is coming from. <grin>

Hurley Dan: Mathely, how old are you? And what's your real name?

Mathely: I'm Cindy, and I'm fifty years old.

Hurley Dan: So at the young age of fifty, Cindy, you are a GREAT-GRANDMA??? How old were you when you had your first child??

Mathely: I was seventeen when my first child was born. I was a grandmother at thirty-five.

Hurley Dan: And what happened to your children's father?

Mathely: He walked off and left me for another woman.

Hurley Dan: Were you ever married, Cindy?

Mathely: I got married a month before I turned sixteen.

Hurley Dan: Did you ever remarry?

Mathely: No, I raised my kids alone because I had heard too many stepparent horror stories. Now I have seven grandchildren and one great-grandchild.

Hurley Dan: And have you changed much from that fifteen-year-old kid who got married?

Mathely: Yes, I have changed completely. Now I am a pharmacy technician and an English major. I never finished high school, but now I am going to college.

Hurley Dan: And Cindy, when you say you want to get married, do you have a steady?

Mathely: Yes I do. He's wonderful. We plan on getting married next year.

Hurley Dan: What kind of setting did you grow up in? Wholesome "Ozzie and Harriet" or what?

Mathely: No, my parents had both been married twice before and separated when I was ten. They never divorced, but dad died a month after I got married.

Hurley Dan: Were you close to your dad? Did it trouble you that he died, Cindy?

Mathely: Yes, it did. I was his only daughter and he never punished me. That was my mom's job. I have always hated it that he never saw any of my children.

Hurley Dan: OK Cindy, I'm ready to write your story. And the title is:

All My Children and Grandchildren and Great-Grandchild Too

Cindy grew up all too quickly.

Or maybe she never grew up till she hit menopause.

She was but fifteen when she married, seventeen when she had her first child, and by the age of fifty, she had seven grandchildren and a great-grandchild too.

She was proud of many things.

She had never finished high school, so in her forties, she obtained a general equivalency diploma and began going to college.

Her married life had never worked out, but finally she found a warm and wonderful man, and together they decided to marry.

But still she had one regret in life that she could never fix. Her dad, who died within a month of her teenage marriage, had never seen any of her children.

Or so she thought. Until one night, when she heard the back door slam, and familiar footsteps wandering into her home. She smelled a forgotten cologne, felt a soft breeze caress her cheek, and knew at last that it was dad all along who had been watching his girl, and all her children, grandchildren, and great-grandchild, too—and keeping them safe.

What the Good Lord Left Behind

Here's one more from November of 1998, about a young woman dealing with the death of her mom and the bankruptcy of her dad.

Hurley Dan: OK, who's next?

SuNKIST: I'm a girl trying to find if family or friends matter more. If what I want, or what I think God wants, matters more.

Hurley Dan: You sound like you must be a teenager?

SuNKIST: Yep.

Hurley Dan: OK, Sun, so what's this about family versus friends?

SuNKIST: We went bankrupt last . . . um . . . August I believe. And lost the house . . . and everything. Dad decided it was a good idea to escape, to move forty-five miles away for the sake of his pride.

Hurley Dan: Wow, Sun, that truly does stink.

SuNKIST: I have the choice this semester to stay with my grandmother there . . . or with my family here. My friend offered me a place with her too, if my grandmother turns me down.

Hurley Dan: Why would your grandma turn you down?

SuNKIST: She's old. My dad doesn't think she'll live long.

Hurley Dan: Would living with your friend be a sound decision? Does this friend live with her parents?

SuNKIST: Yes, but living with a friend complicates a
friendship.

Hurley Dan: Is the friend a girl (I hope)?

SuNKIST: Yeah.

Hurley Dan: Would you guys be able to compensate the
family in any financial way for putting you up?

SuNKIST: Yes. I'm pretty sure.

Hurley Dan: So how are you feeling about all this?

SuNKIST: Trying to get through.

Hurley Dan: There's MUCH worse things than money problems. (Like health problems. Marital problems. Loss of a
loved one.)

SuNKIST: Yah. Had some of those as well.

Hurley Dan: YOU DID??? Like what other problems, Sun?

SuNKIST: Lost my mom when I was nine. Car accident.
My dad has been in the hospital, too, for a heart attack.

Hurley Dan: Sun!!! OK, everybody in the room, GROUP HUG FOR SUN!!!!

Bergan: (((((Sun)))))

FERNE: (((((((((((hug)))))))))))

LC81: (((((((((((((((((((((((Sun))))))))))))))))))))))))))

SuNKIST: ::squeezed to death with hugs:: thanks guys:)

Hurley Dan: Sun, this is beyond all odds. Mom dies in freak accident. Dad is seriously ill and goes bankrupt. How does all this happen to one kid???

SuNKIST: Ask myself the same thing. There's gotta be a reason. But I wouldn't believe in God as much had I not been through it all.

Hurley Dan: What was you mom like, Sun? What kind of memories do you have of her?

SuNKIST: She was fun. I remember she'd come home from midnight shifts, and it didn't keep her down. We'd go to the waterfalls and have breakfast. Play tag. Everything. She was a kid. She was stressed a lot, though. Clinical depression. Which she lovingly passed on to me.

Hurley Dan: Why do you put it that way? "Lovingly" passed onto you?

SuNKIST: Sarcastic.

Hurley Dan: But it sounds like she was pretty loving, yes?

SuNKIST: Very much so. But there were times it was hard with her. She was stressed so much, and worked a lot.

Hurley Dan: So how are you doing now?

SuNKIST: Shaky. It's up and down. Like everyone else I guess. Sometimes I couldn't be any happier. But sometimes I get pretty bitter.

Hurley Dan: Ok, Sun. I'm ready to write your story. And here it comes. The title is:

What the Good Lord Left Behind

On the day of Sunny's birth, her Mom and Dad knew they had been blessed.

It was a day like no other, an experience that forever changed them.

They saw this perfect being, this creation of pure beauty and joy. From that day forward, they dedicated themselves to giving her all they could give.

But sometimes they didn't have all they wanted to give. Sunny's mom wanted so much to be sitting at home with her, instead of working. She wanted so much to be always happy, to be giving Sunny the kind of happy home she deserved.

Sometimes she succeeded, sometimes she could not.

But Mom and Dad did all they could with what the good Lord had given them.

And then, one day, the good Lord took back what He had given.

He took Sunny's mom back to heaven. He took the health of Sunny's dad.

He took back the money and success and home that had been theirs.

But the good Lord left behind one thing.

There, in the clarity that had been so pure and holy on her day of birth, was the love that her parents had always felt for her.

This love is the staff and the rod of Sunny's strength.

This love is the one thing that so many kids with their cars and their clothes always wanted, but never had.

This love Sunny has had since the day she was born, and always will have.

Nothing shall ever take away from her this love that conquers all.

One Last Minute

Considering that my "Amazing Instant Novelist" site is still going strong, I like to remember the words of that doubter who told me it would never work. They remind me to never, ever let the skeptics, the people who laugh, stop me. I'm going to keep following my dream of writing one-on-one stories for people. And I have yet another crazy quest in mind right now: to travel the globe, trekking to villages in Africa and the Amazon, to street corners in Vietnam and Venice, with only a typewriter and a translator, hearing people's stories and giving one in return—in a sense, to go 'round the world in 60 seconds.

If they're anything like the 22,613 I've heard in America, I have a hunch what I'll find.

Six billion stories.

One heart.

About the Author

Dan Hurley began wearing bow ties at a very early age.

Within a few months of turning thirteen in 1970, Dan became a hippie kid, reading everything he could get his hands on that smacked of "cool," "heavy" and "far out."

At Beloit College in Wisconsin, Dan formed a musical trio called the Mutations, performing such original compositions as "Electrocution," "Welcome to the Atomic Age," and of course who could forget, "I Hate You." He graduated with a degree in English Composition and Philosophy in 1979.

In addition to his sixteen-year career as the world's only 60-Second Novelist, Dan has been a freelance journalist since 1980, beginning with his article in the *National Examiner*, "I Was Attacked by Killer Bigfoot."

Dan has since served as a contributing editor of *Psychology Today* and *Health Confidential*, and as senior writer for the *Medical Tribune*. He has published hundreds of articles and essays in *Family Circle*, *The New York Times*, *People*, *TV Guide*, *New York*, *Good Housekeeping*, *Woman's Day*, *McCall's*, *American Health* and many more. In 1995 he won the American Society of Journalists and Authors' Donald Robinson Memorial Award for Investigative Journalism. He currently serves as ASJA's vice president for publications.

In Person or Online

When he isn't writing 60-Second Novels on sidewalks, in cornfields or from rooftops, Dan Hurley writes them at parties, trade shows and special events for corporations, colleges, department stores, casinos and individuals. His clients have included AT&T, Metropolitan Life, IBM, Lucent, Macy's, Bloomingdale's, Trump Plaza in Atlantic City, Harrah's in Las Vegas, Merrill Lynch, Seton Hall University, the University of Portland and many people you've never heard of. For information:

Novel Products Inc.
P.O. Box 43488
Upper Montclair, NJ 07043
fax 973-744-5024

You can also visit Dan's "Amazing Instant Novelist" site, the #1 writing site online with over 5 million hits per month. Enter writing contests; share your own stories, poems, memoirs, opinions, humor and more; read Dan's daily novels; take courses; join Dan's "Amazing Writers' Group;" chat with fellow writers, and order your own personal 60-Second Novel from Dan. Visit the Amazing Instant Novelist at:

AOL keyword: novel
www.instantnovelist.com
e-mail: instantnovelist@aol.com

The Love of Knowledge

ARISTOTLE
WOULD HAVE LIKED
OPRAH

LESSONS FOR LIVING
AND OTHER
PHILOSOPHIC MUSINGS
ETHEL DIAMOND

Code #7206 • $10.95

From its birth in ancient Greece to the present day, philosophy has inspired us with insightful questions and thoughts to help us live life to the fullest.

This book will give you the basic tenets for many of the most important thinkers throughout history and show you how they relate directly to our everyday life. From advertising slogans to celebrities, to familiar phrases, you'll be amazed at how much of our popular culture results from the teachings of the great philosophers.

A New Season of
Chicken Soup for the Soul

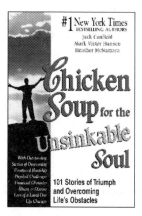